Funny Pets

Vol. 2

GRAYSCALE PHOTO COLORING BOOK FOR ADULTS

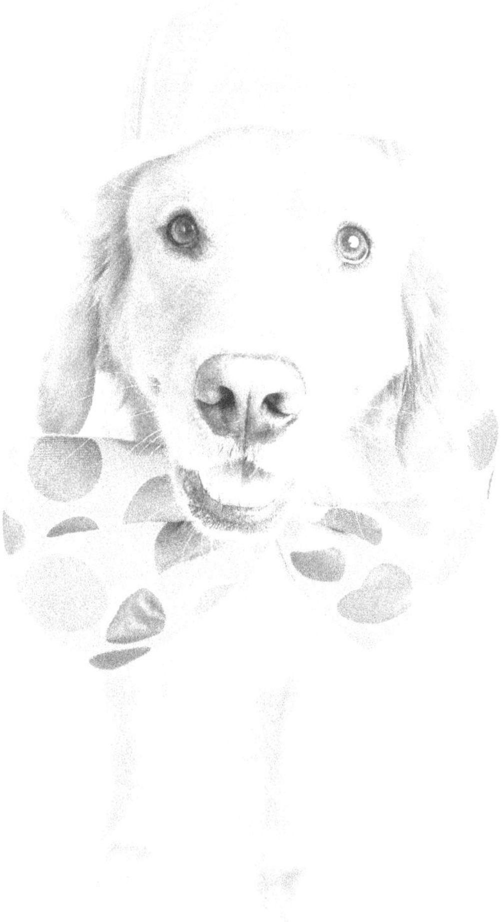

Majestic COLORING

www.MajesticColoring.com

ISBN: 978-1532859595

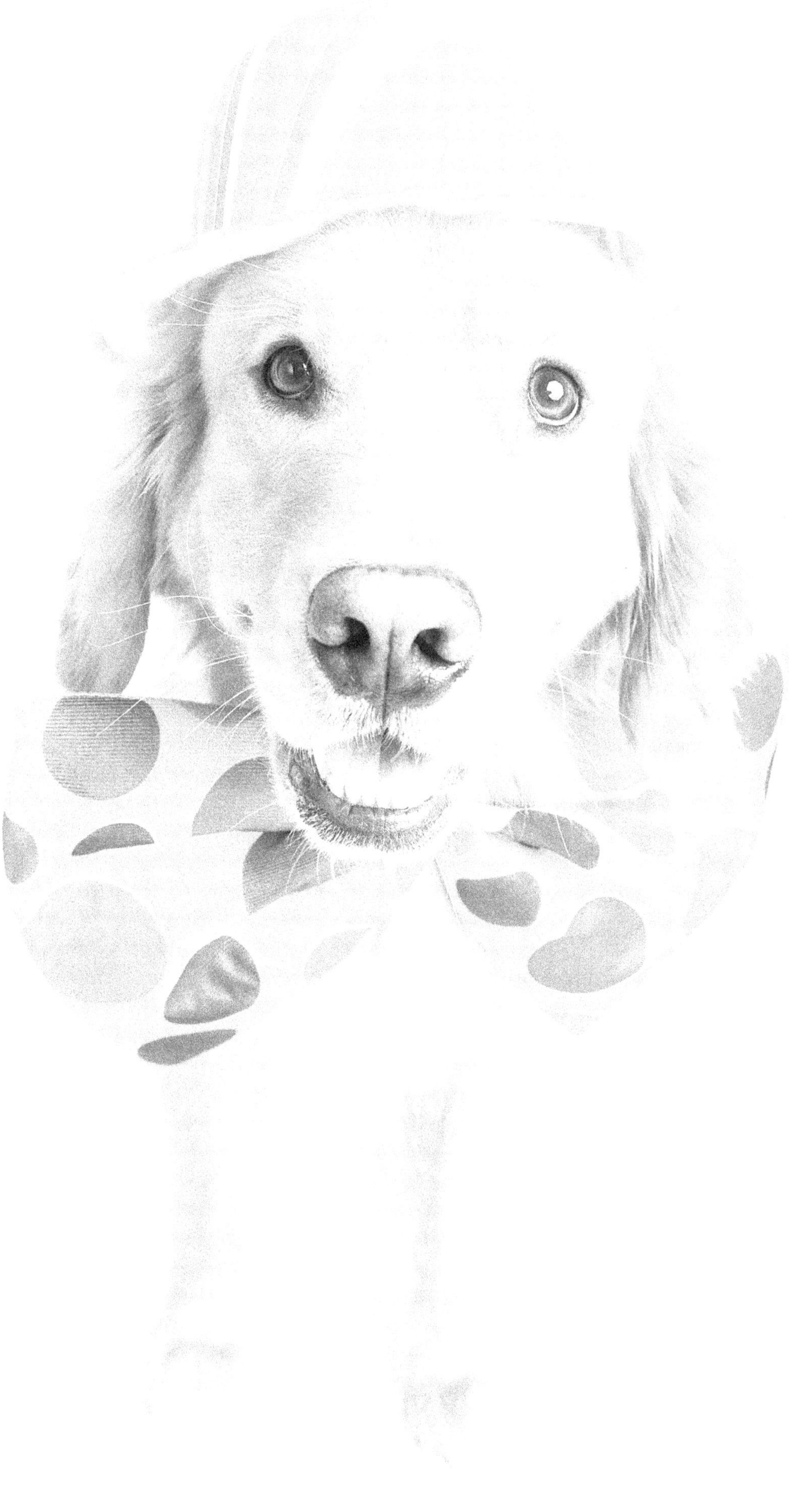

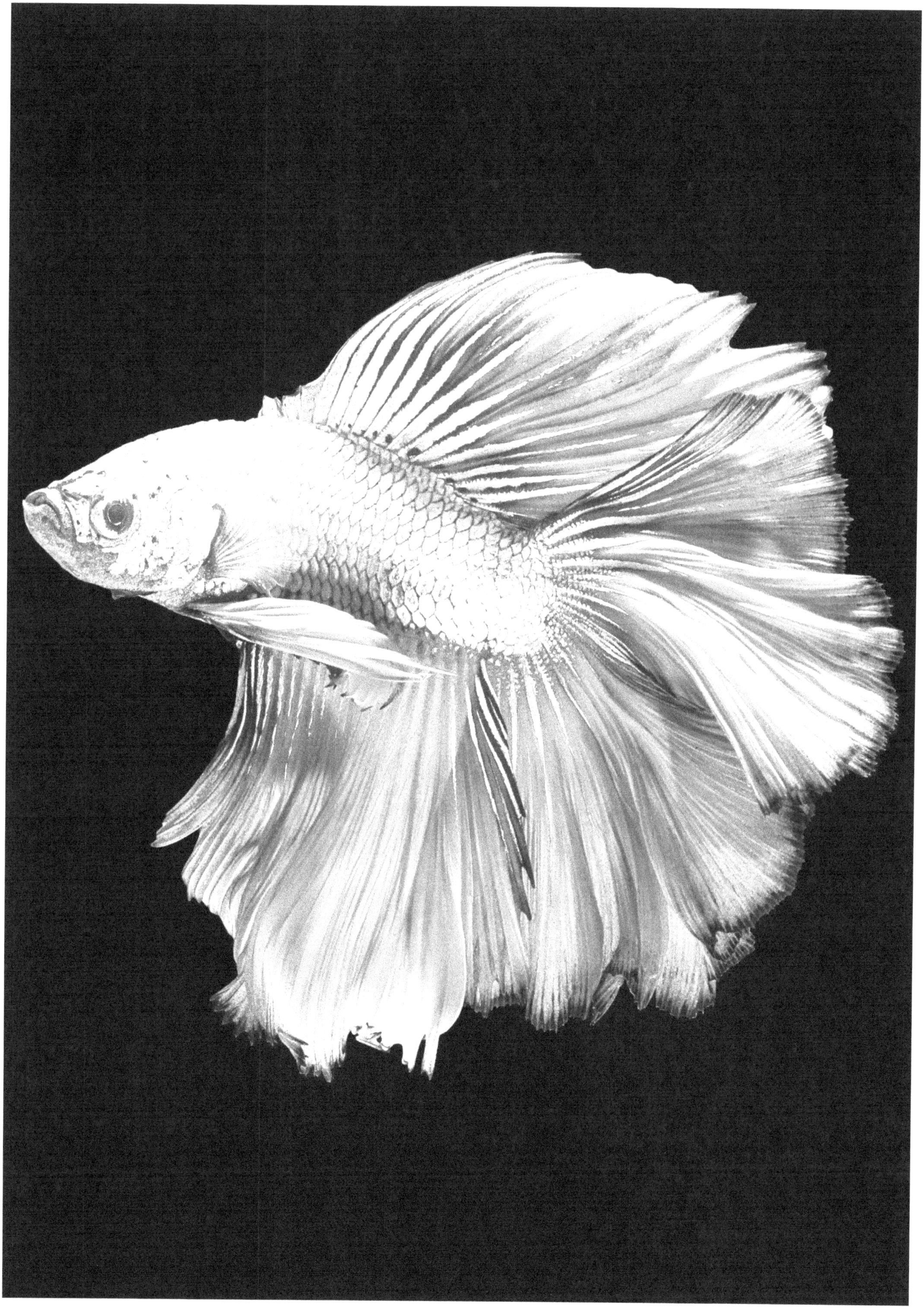

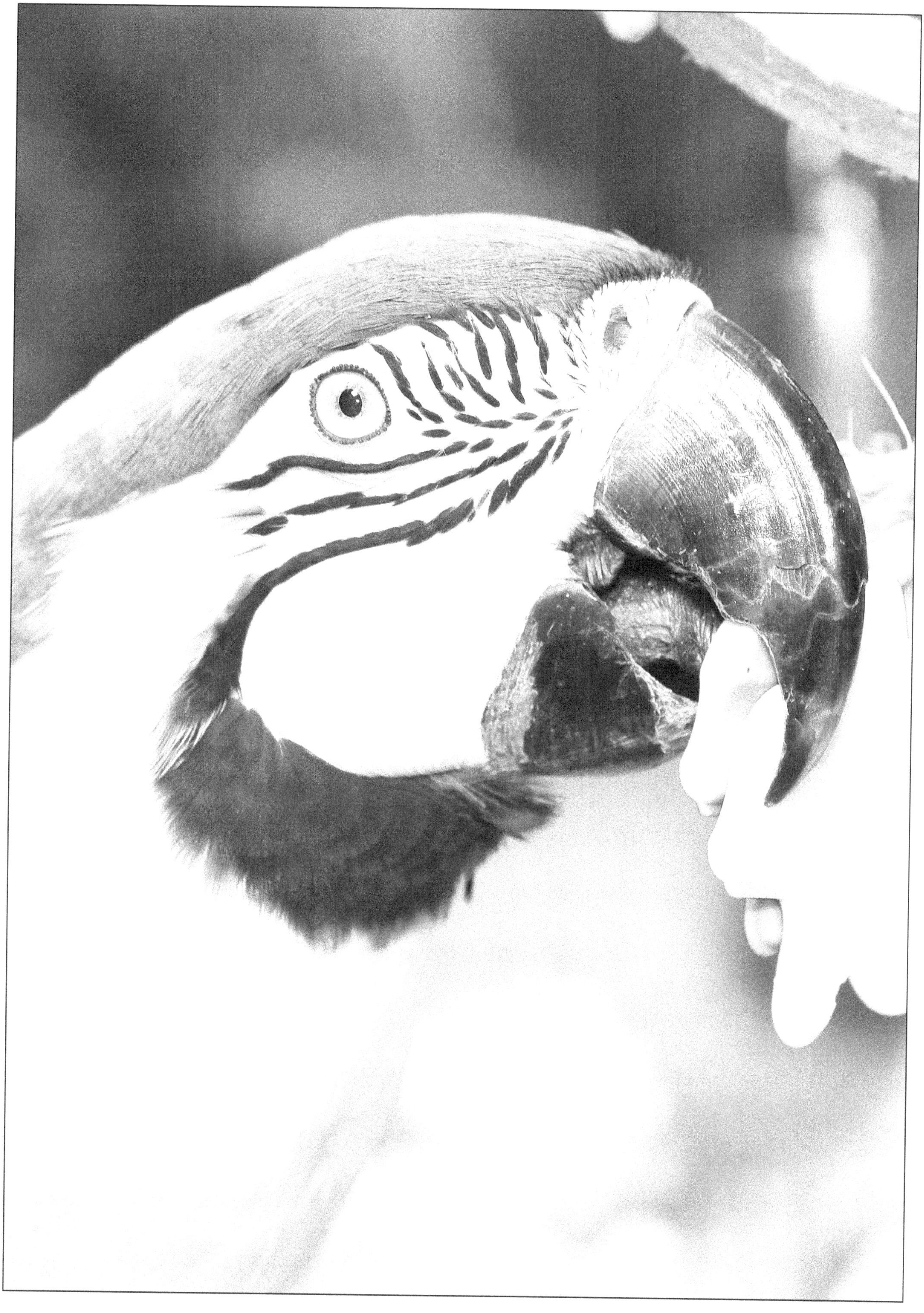

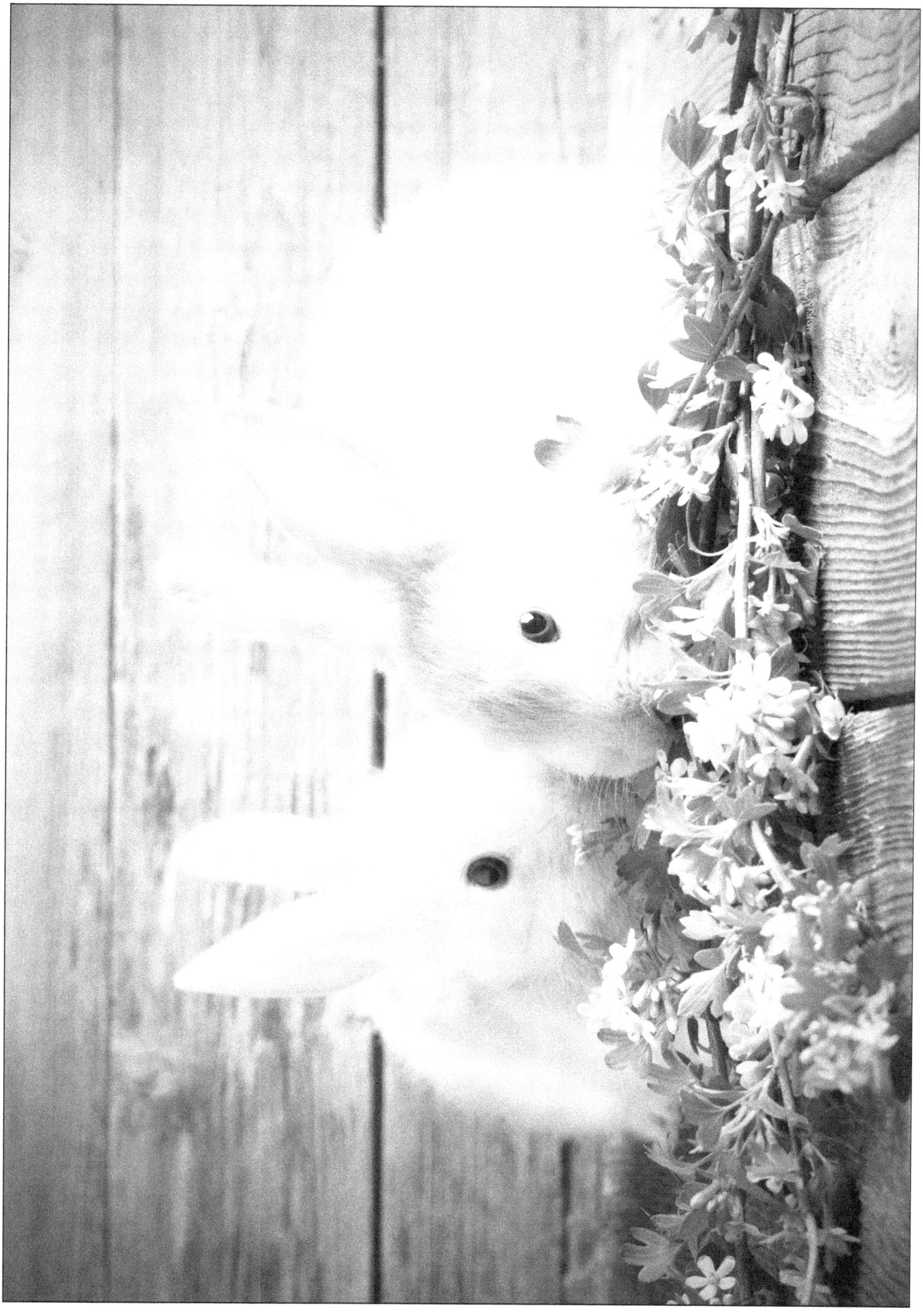

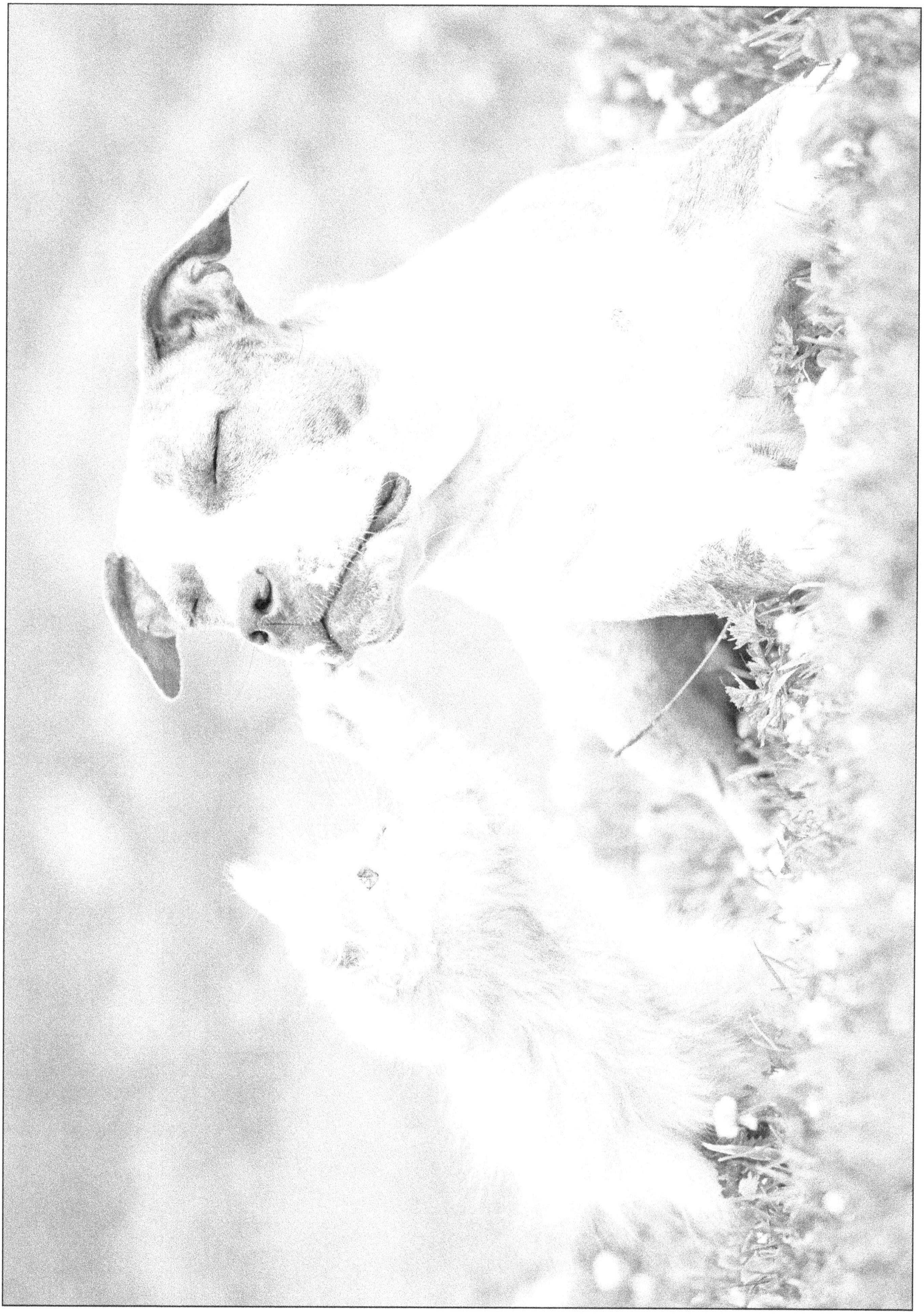

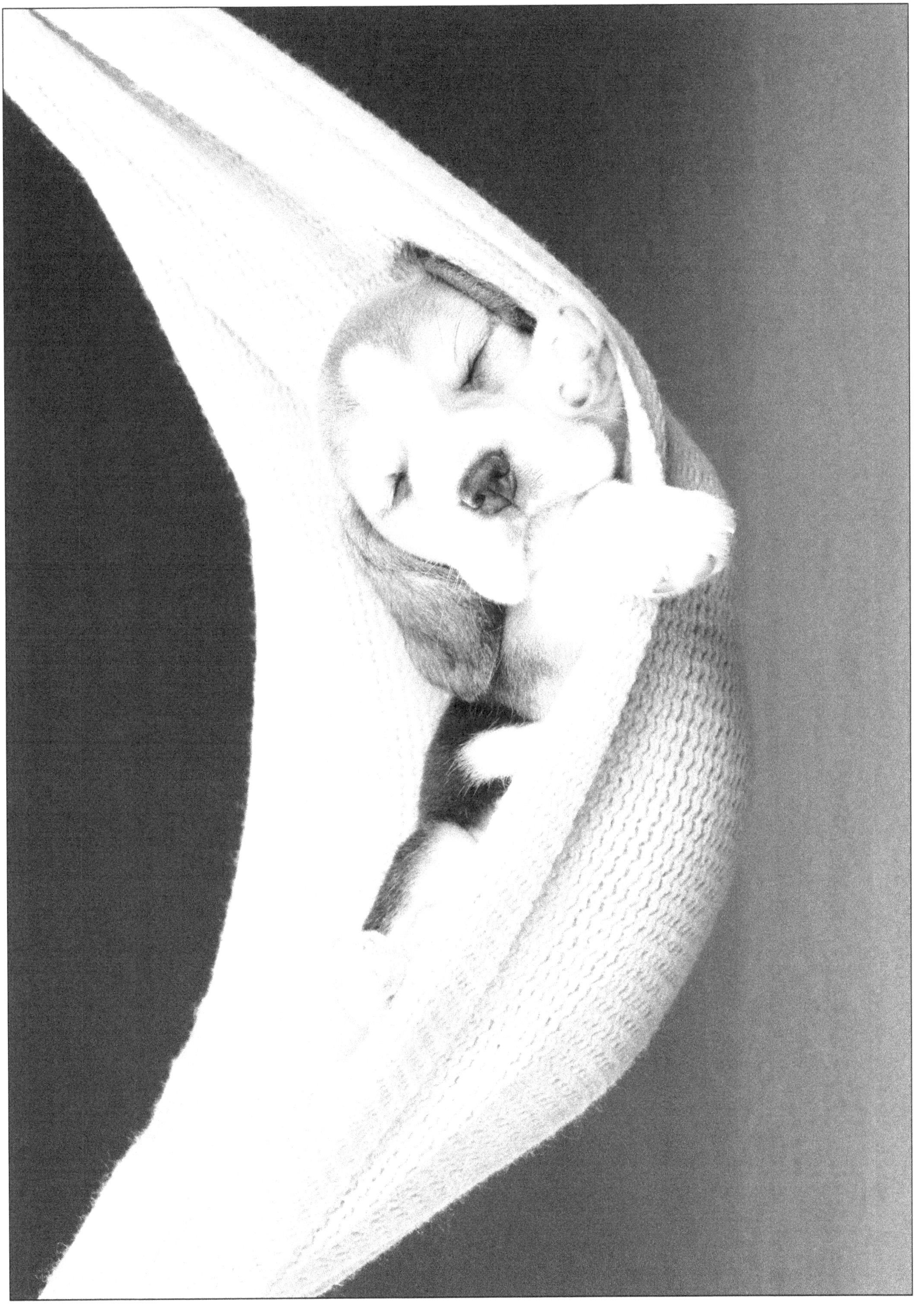

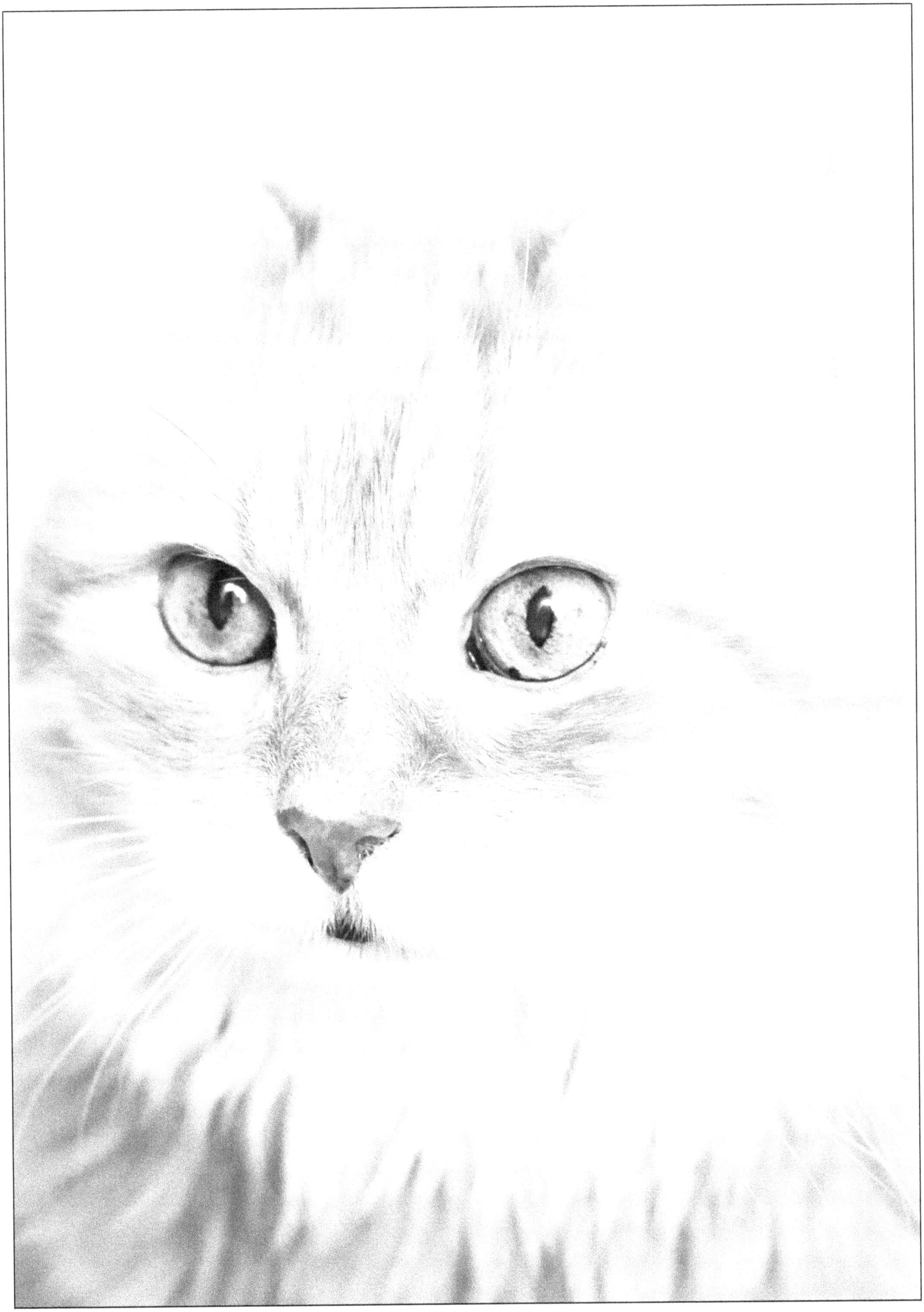

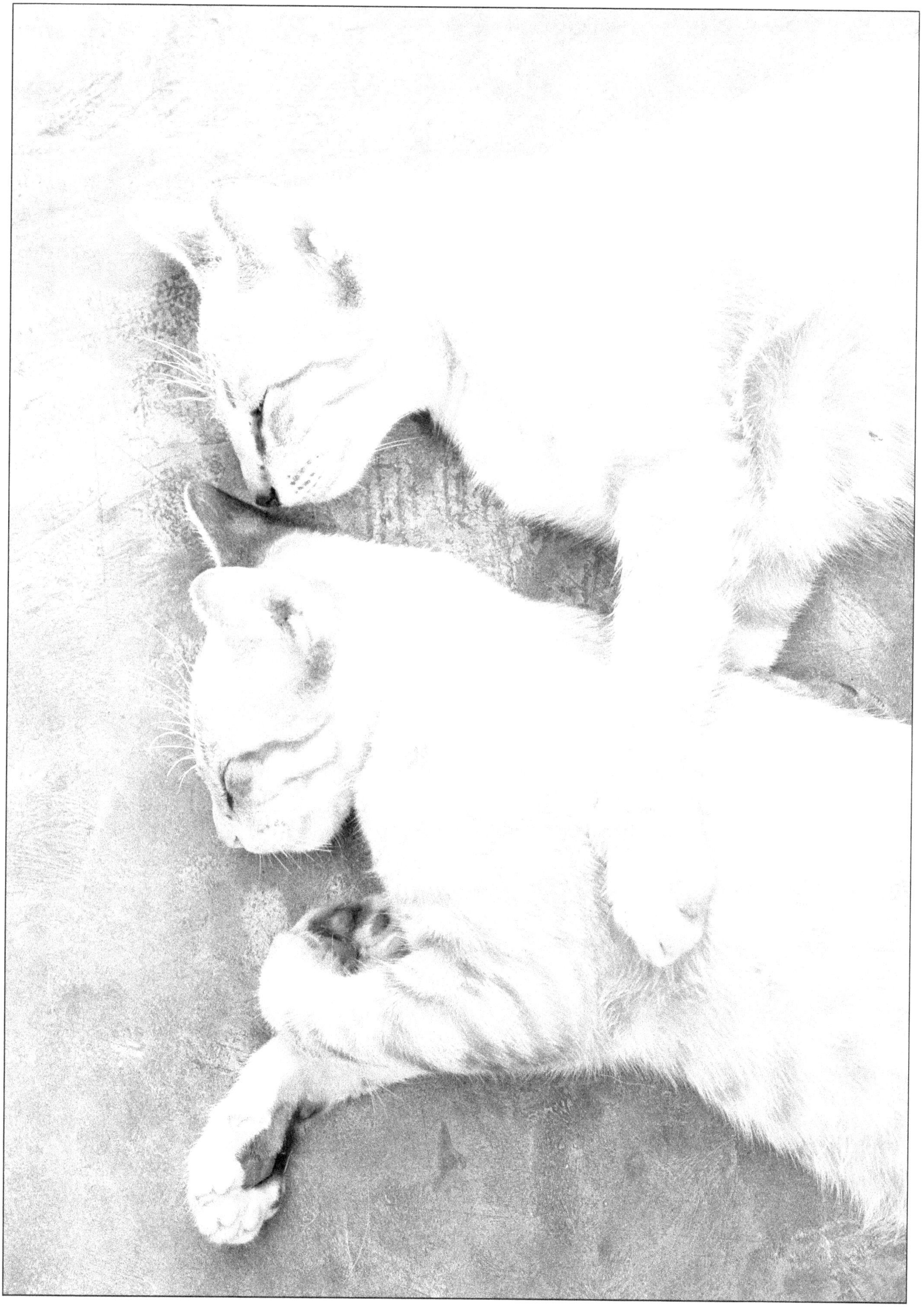

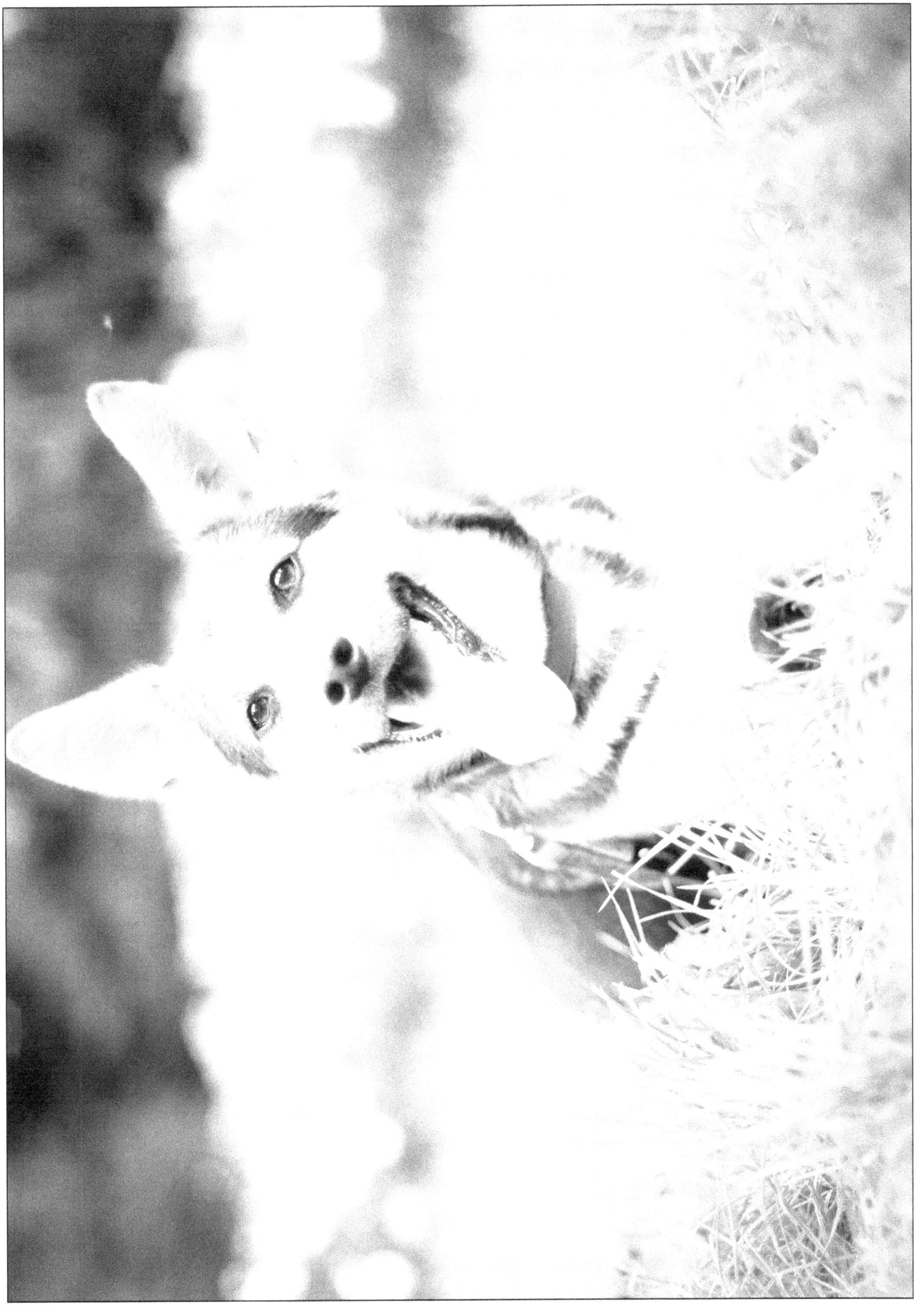

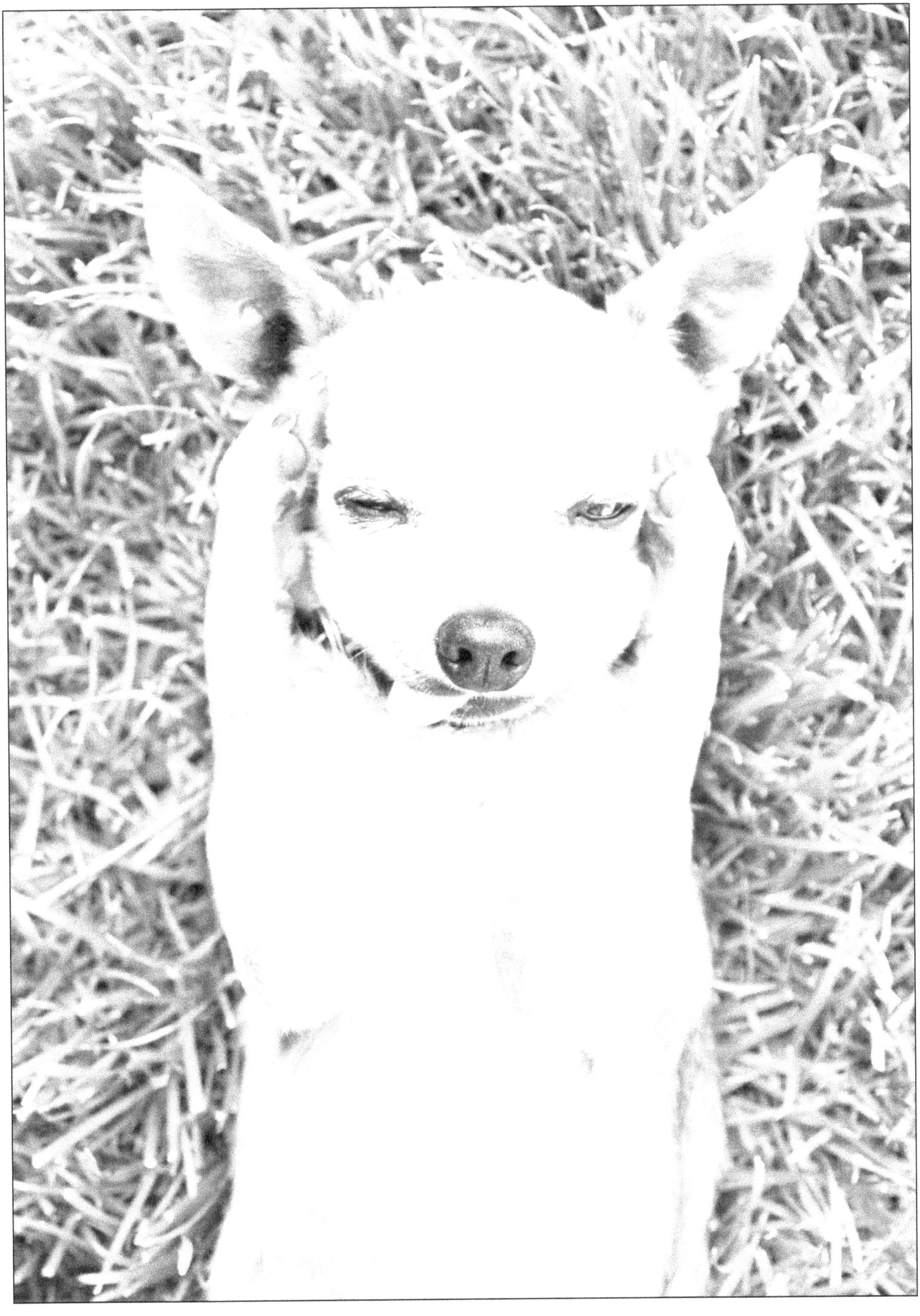

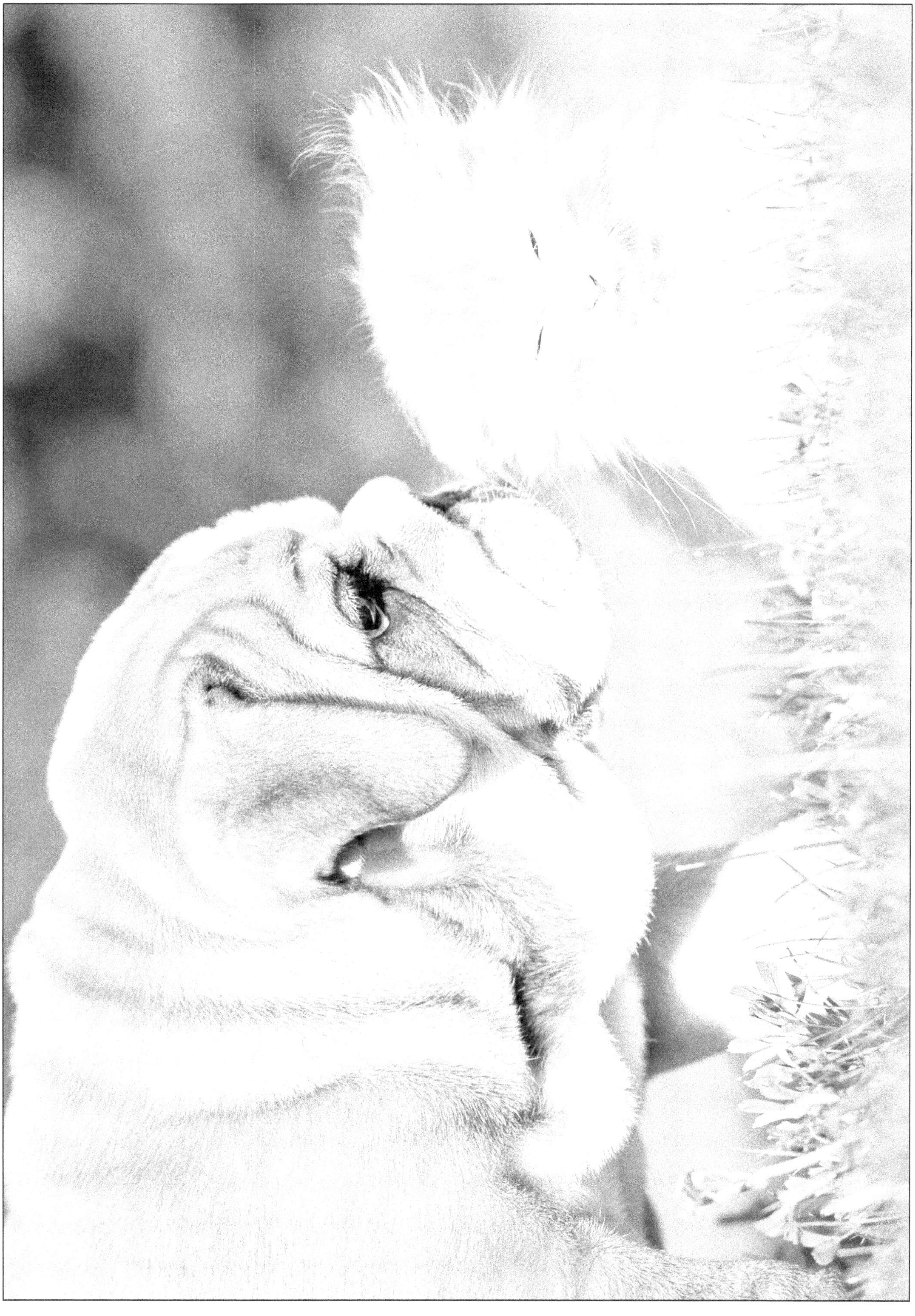

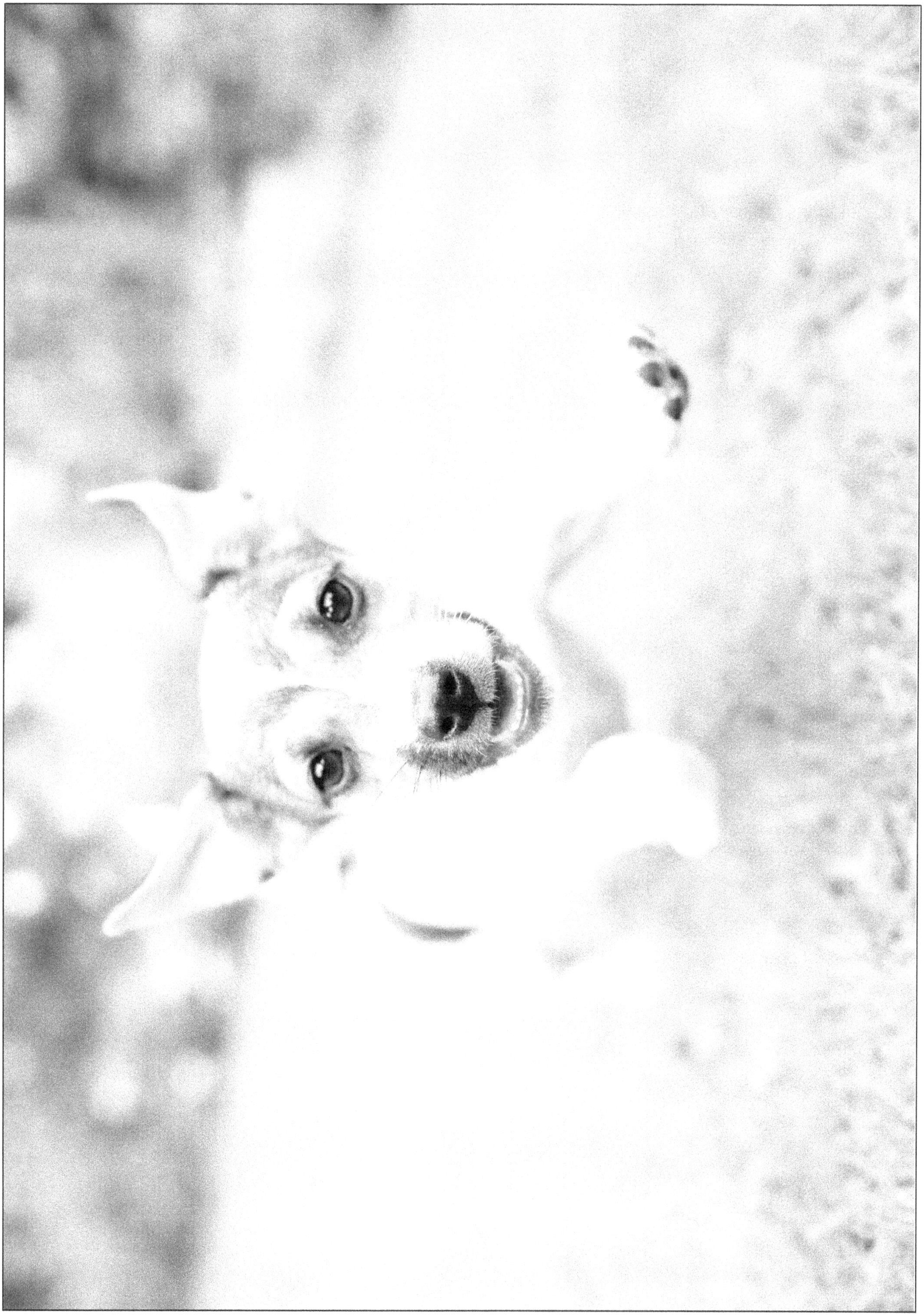

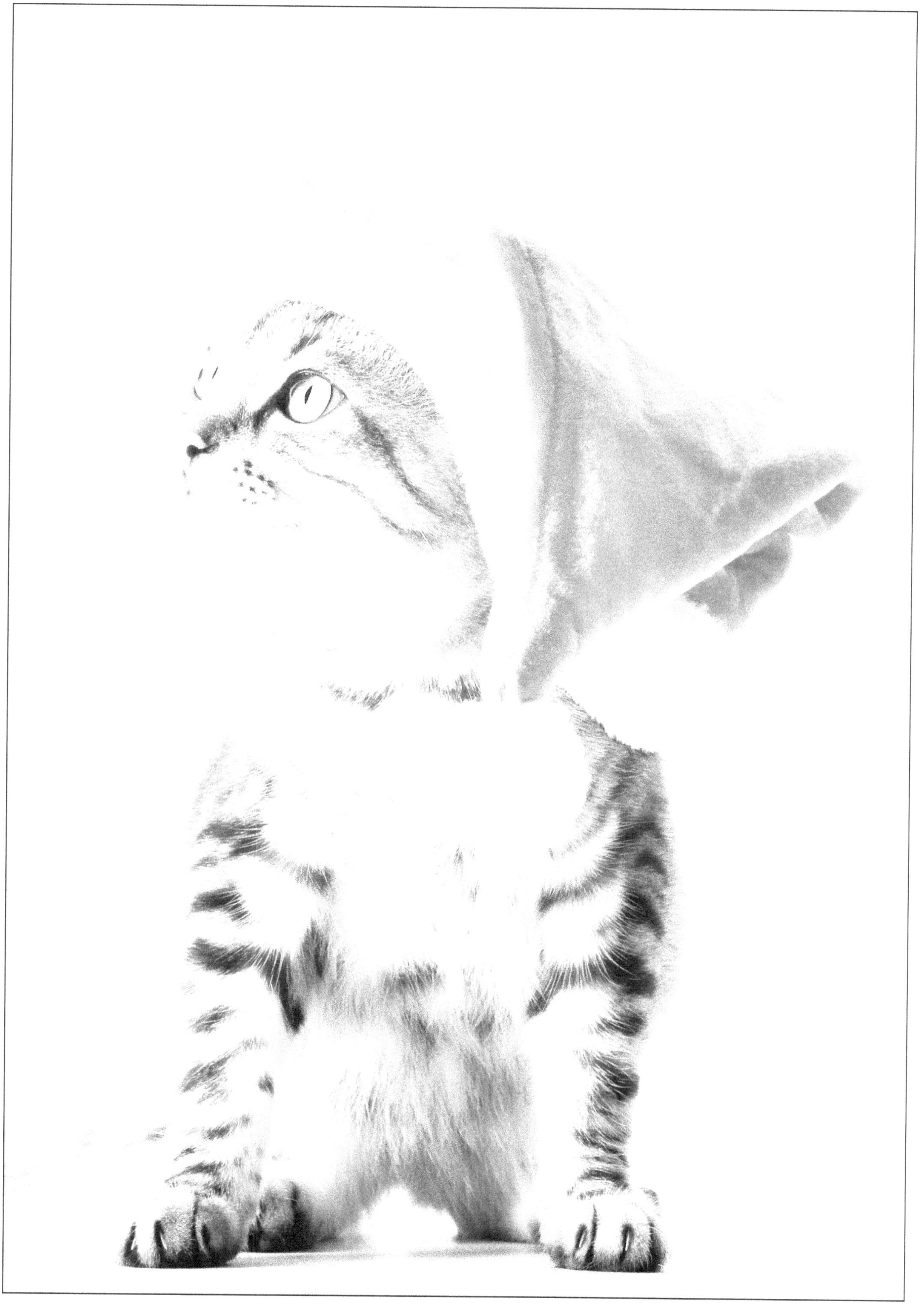

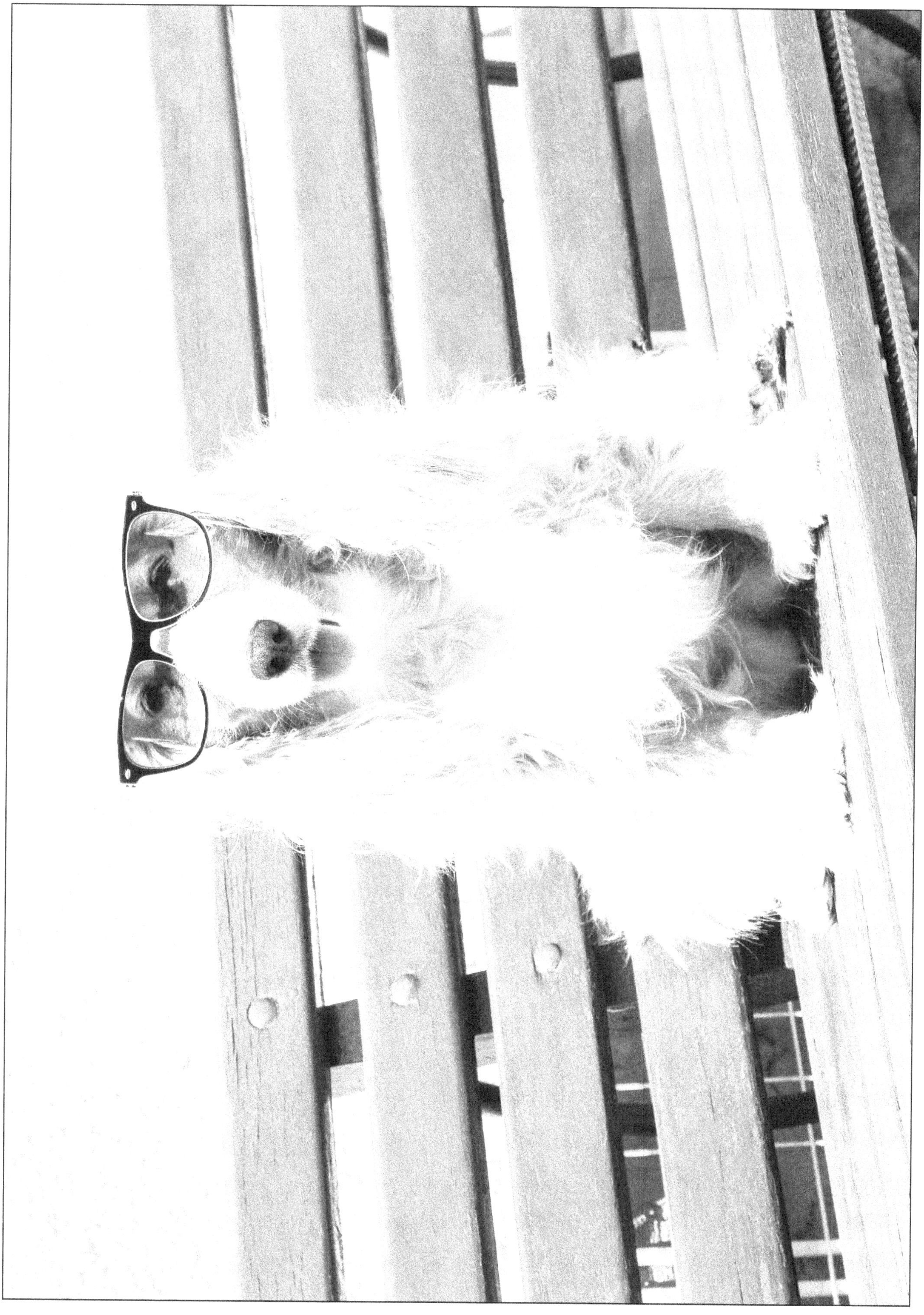

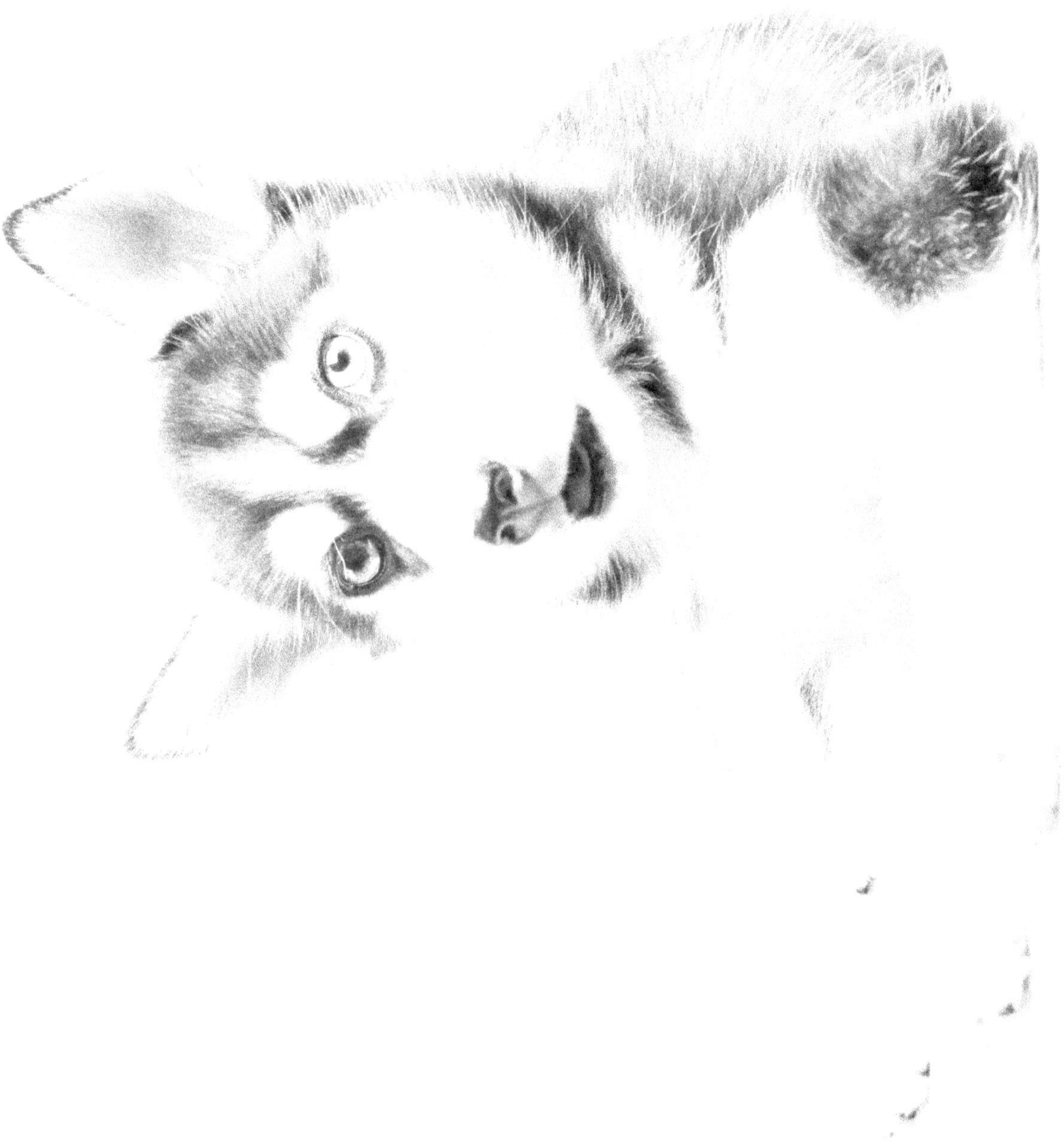

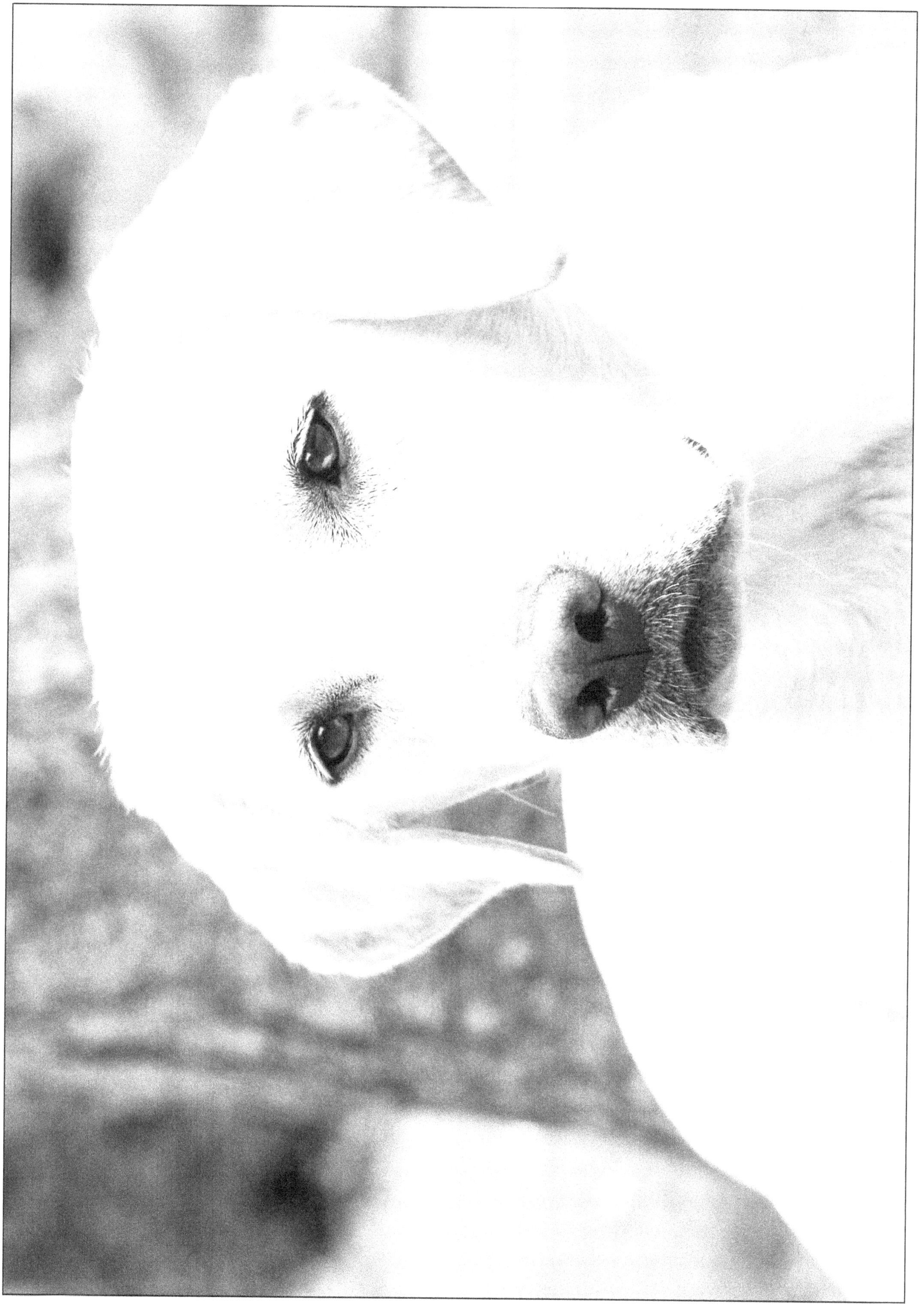

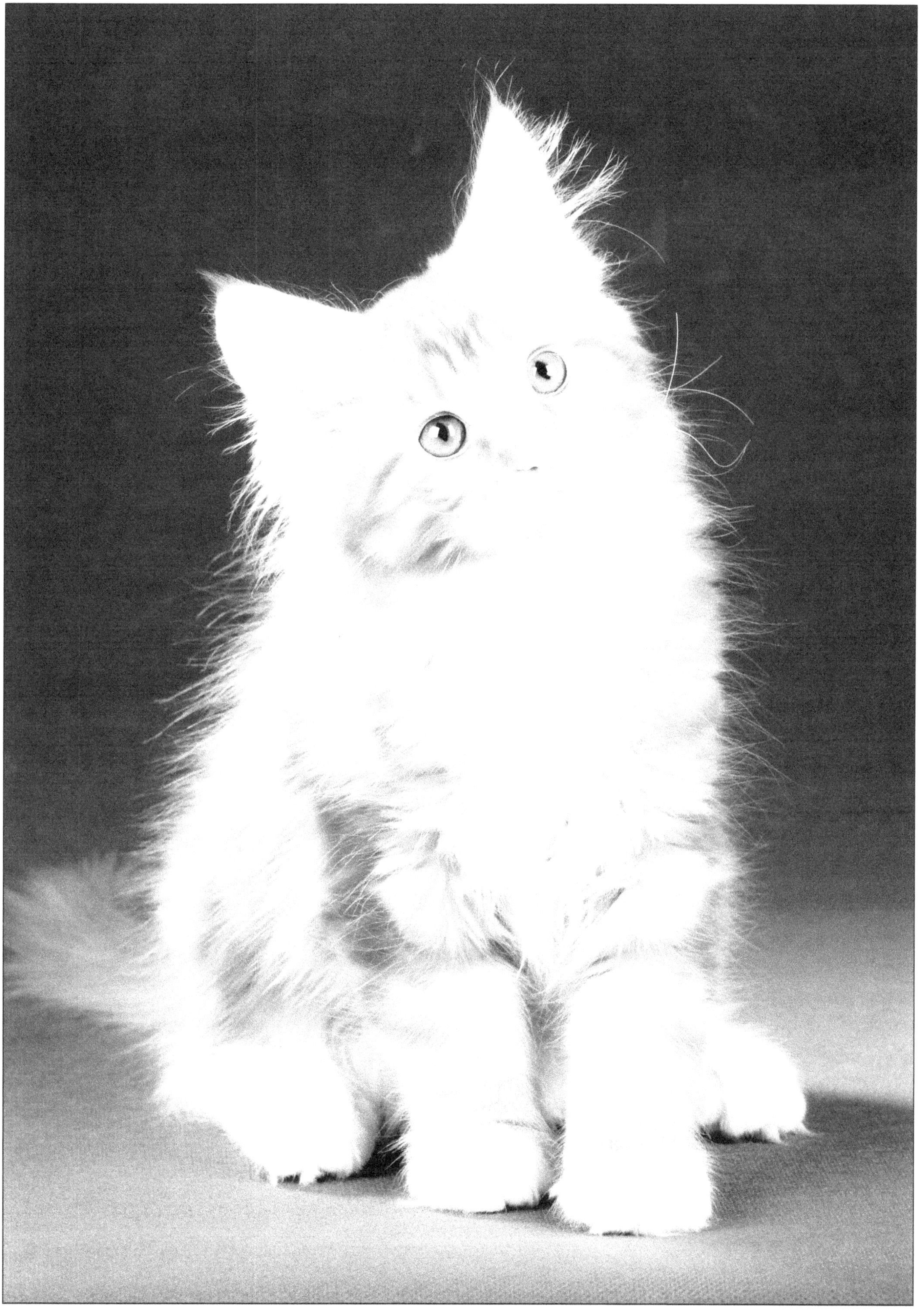

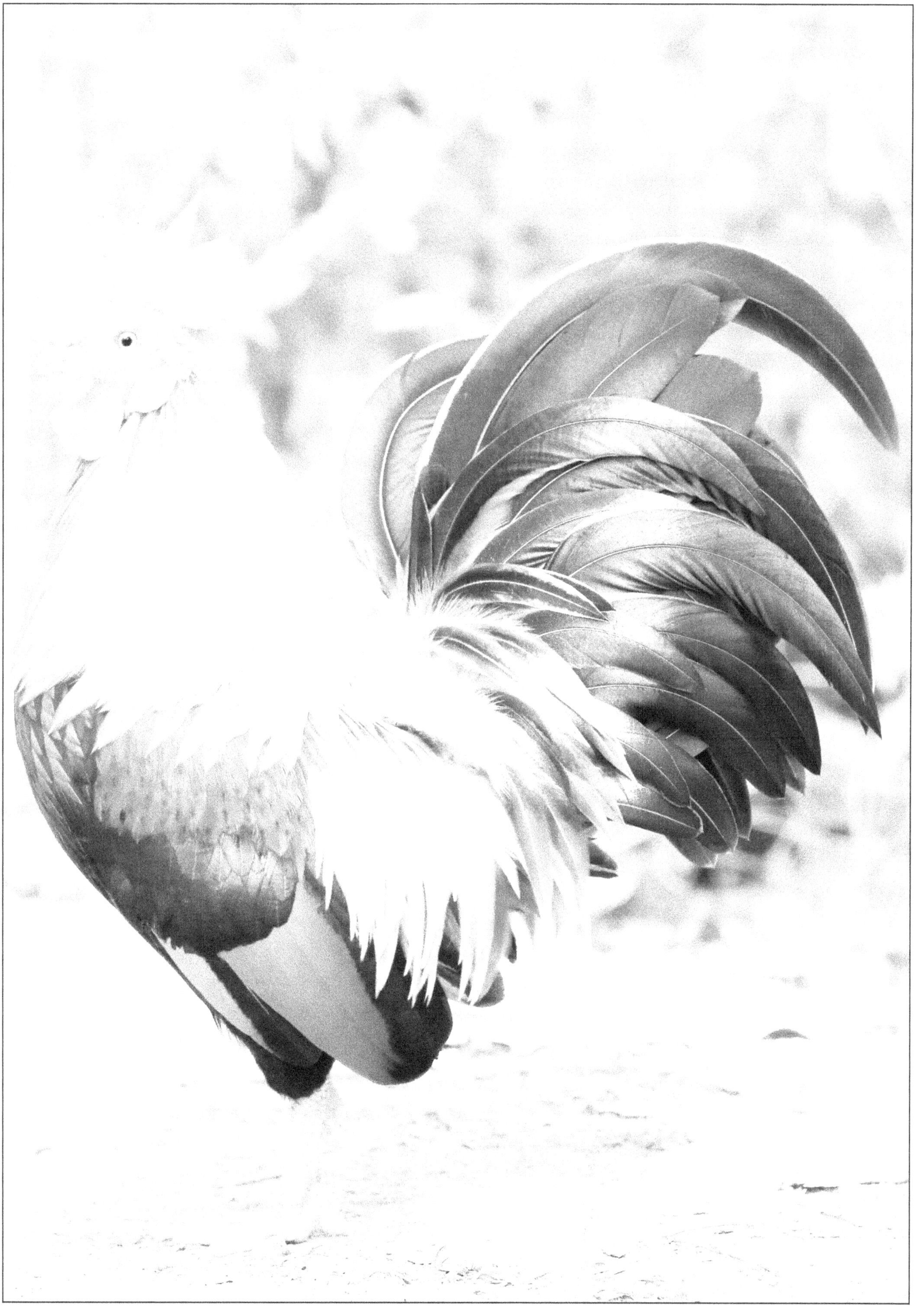

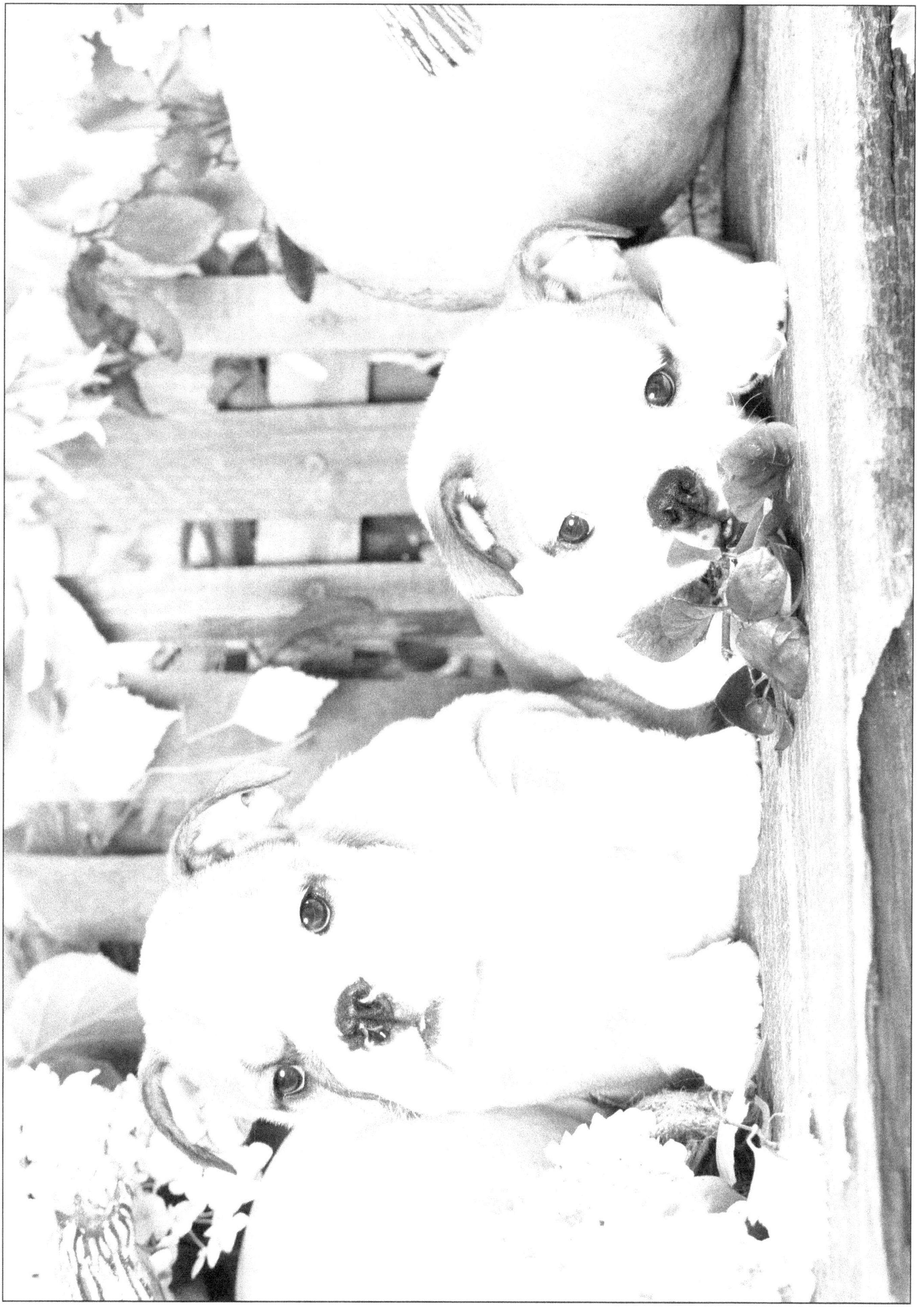

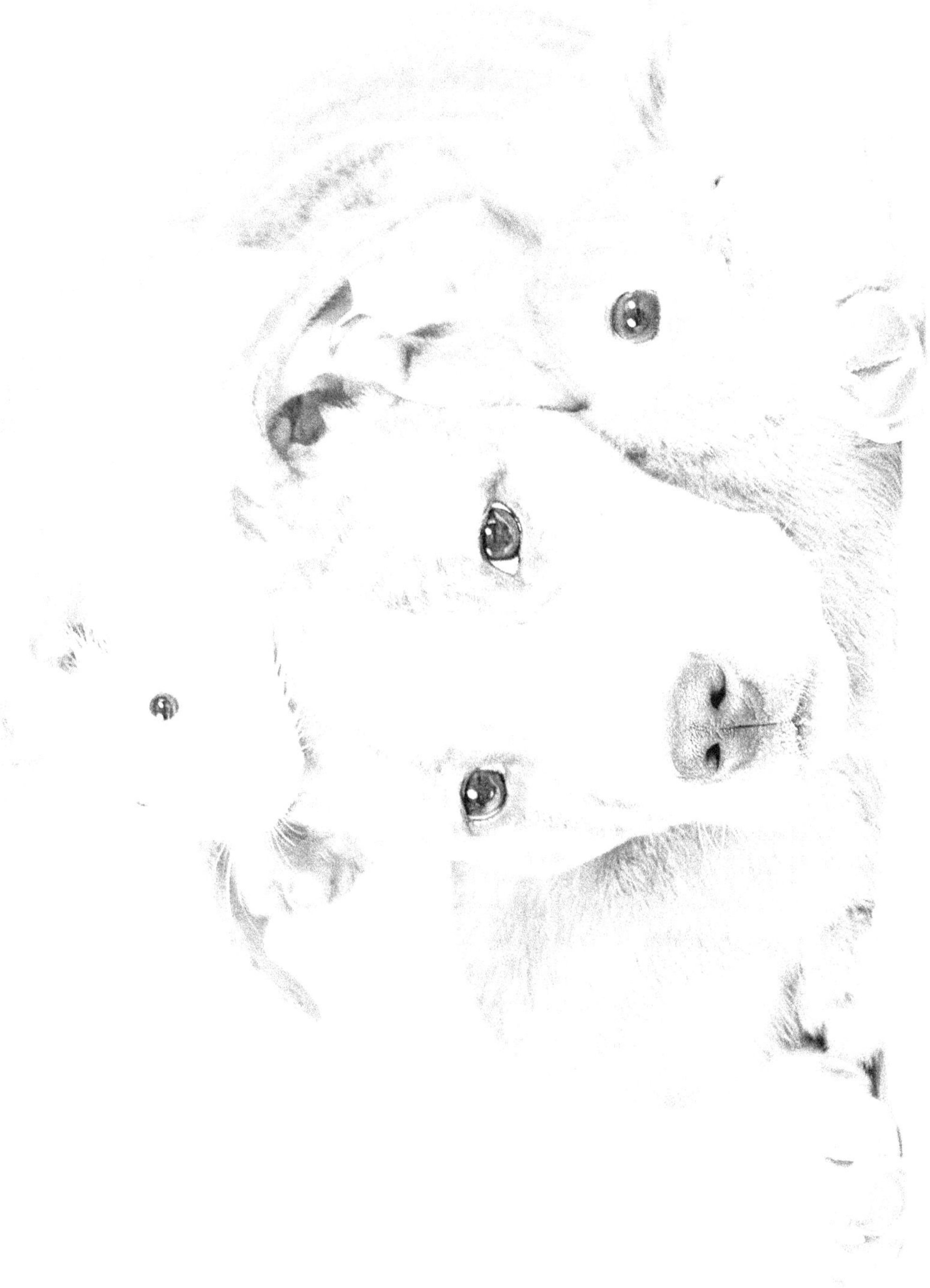

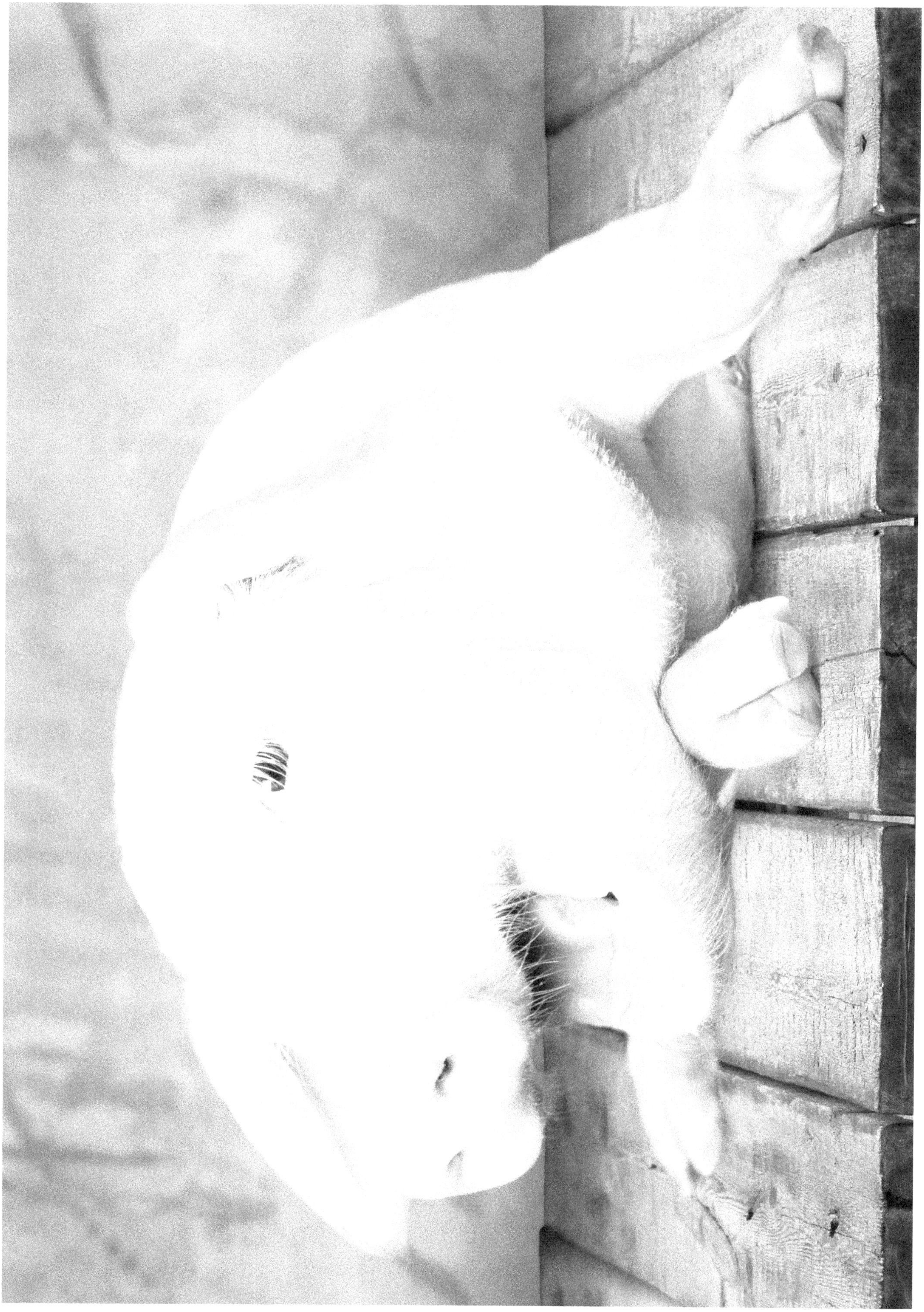

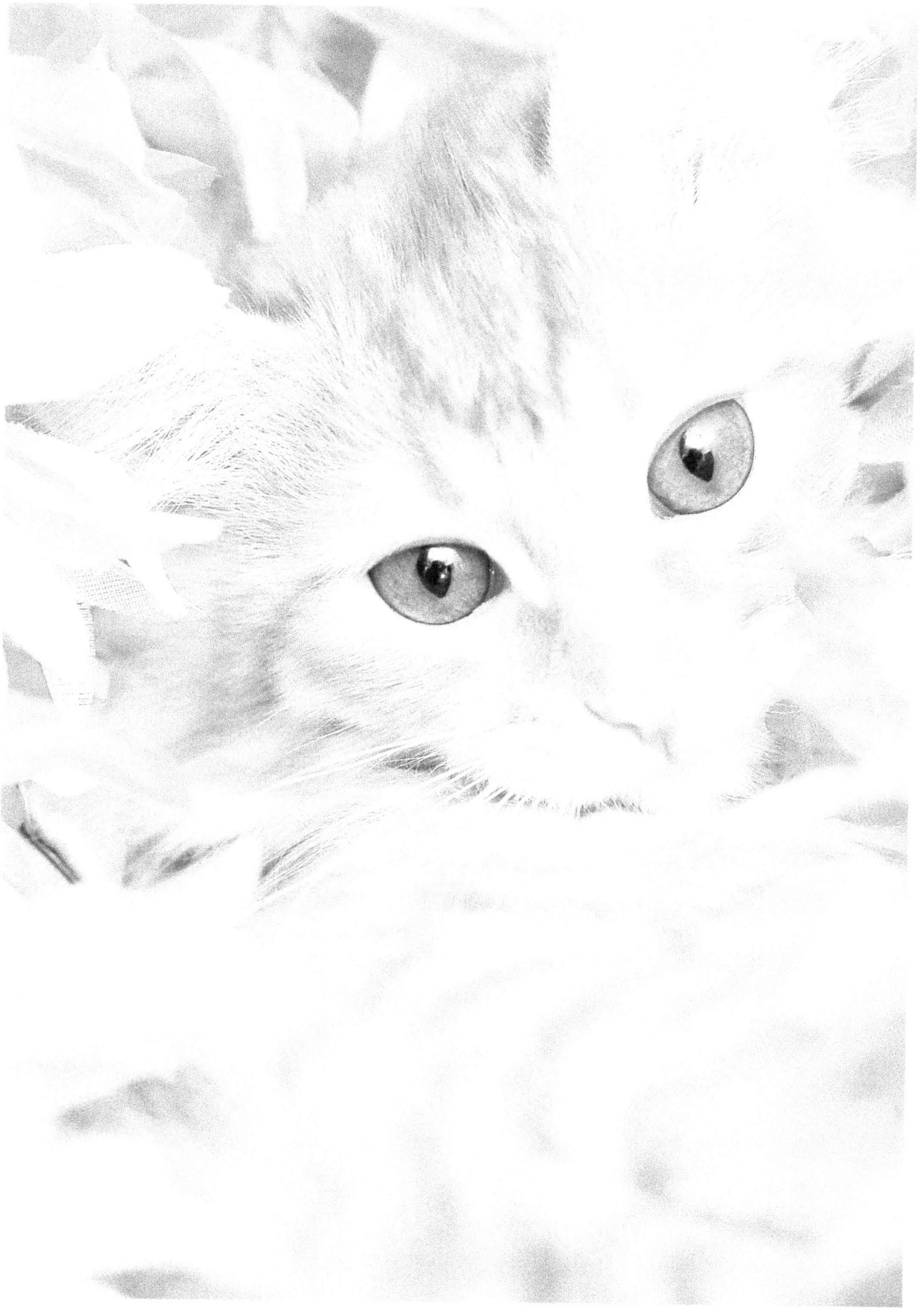

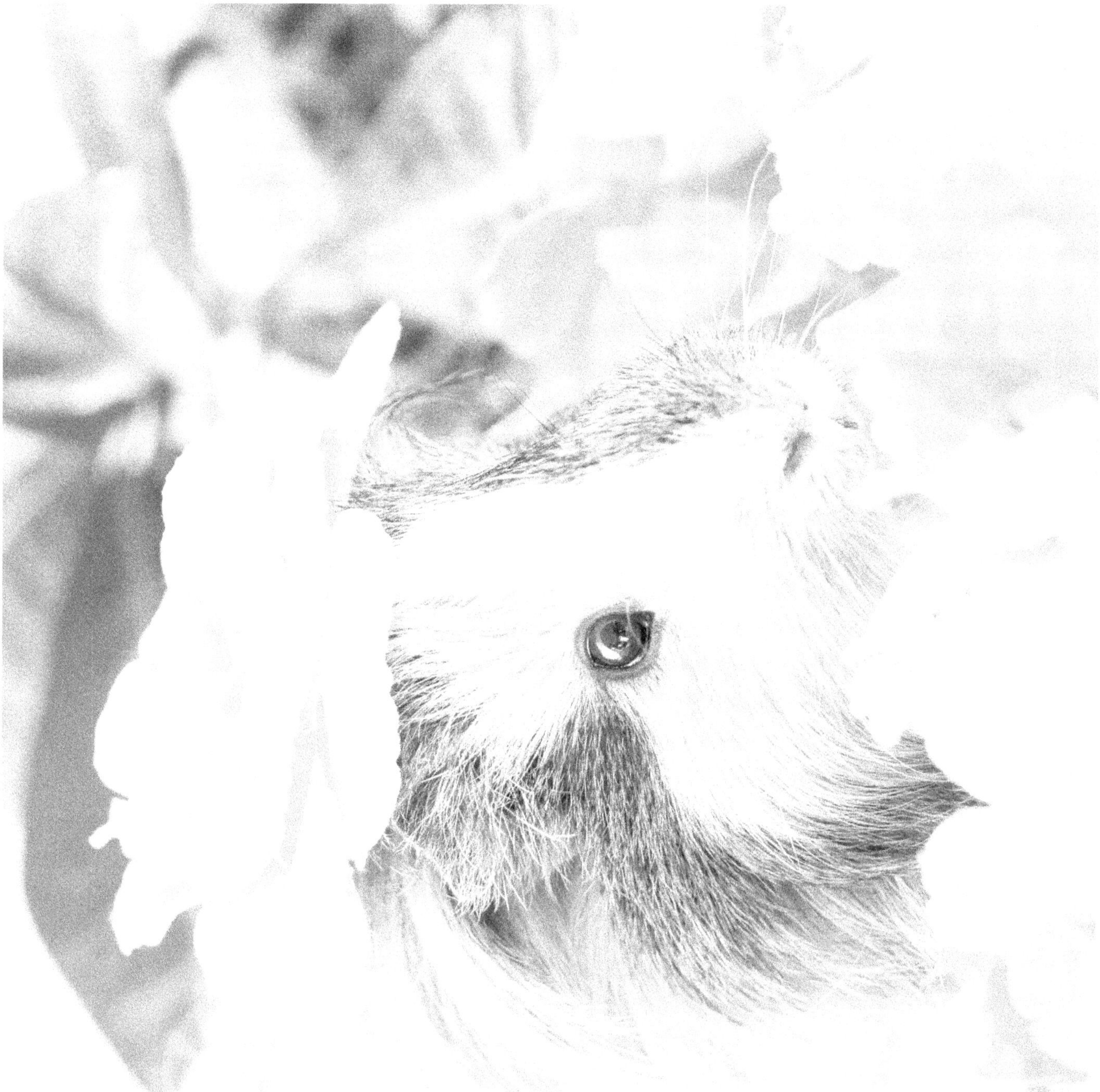

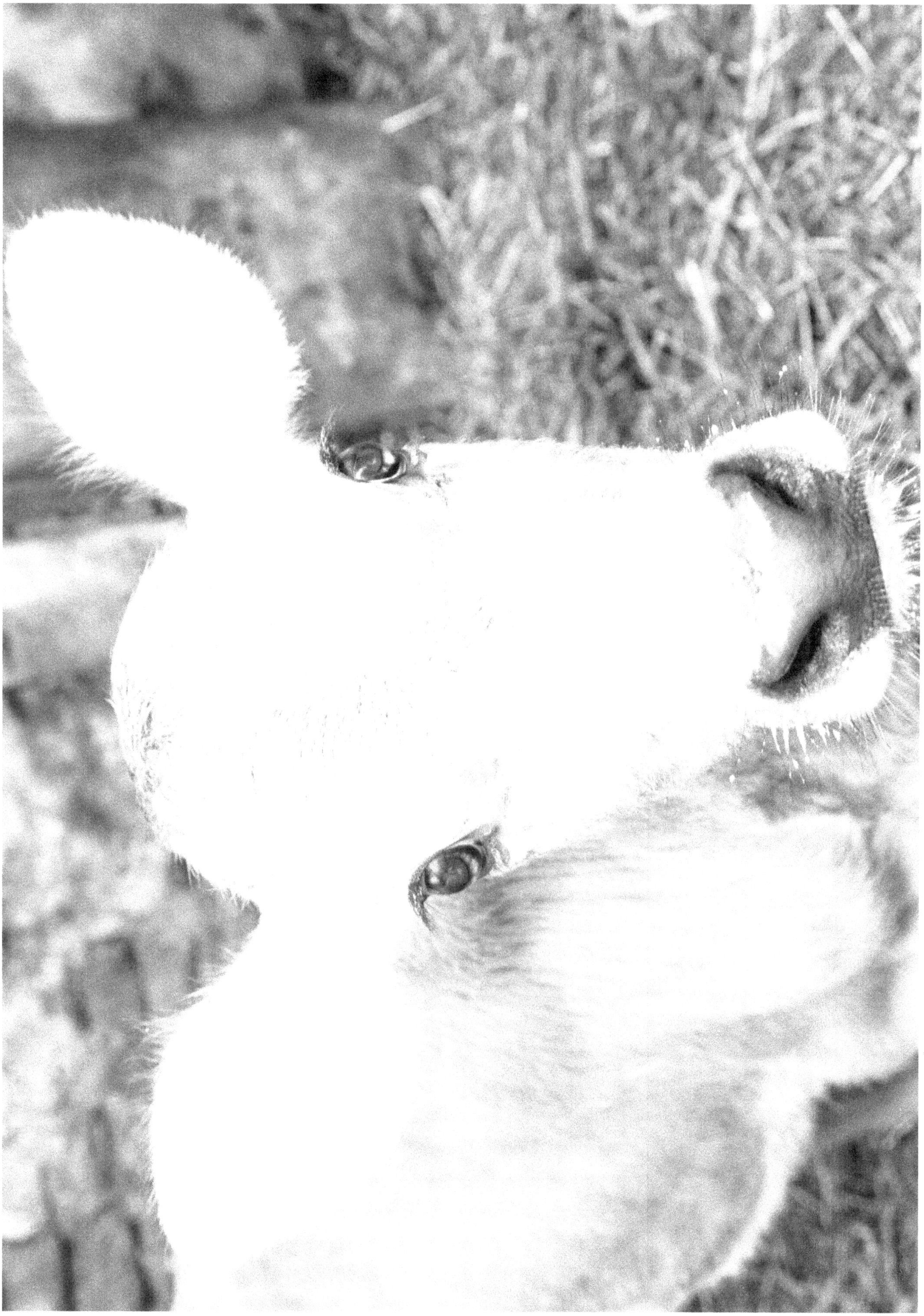

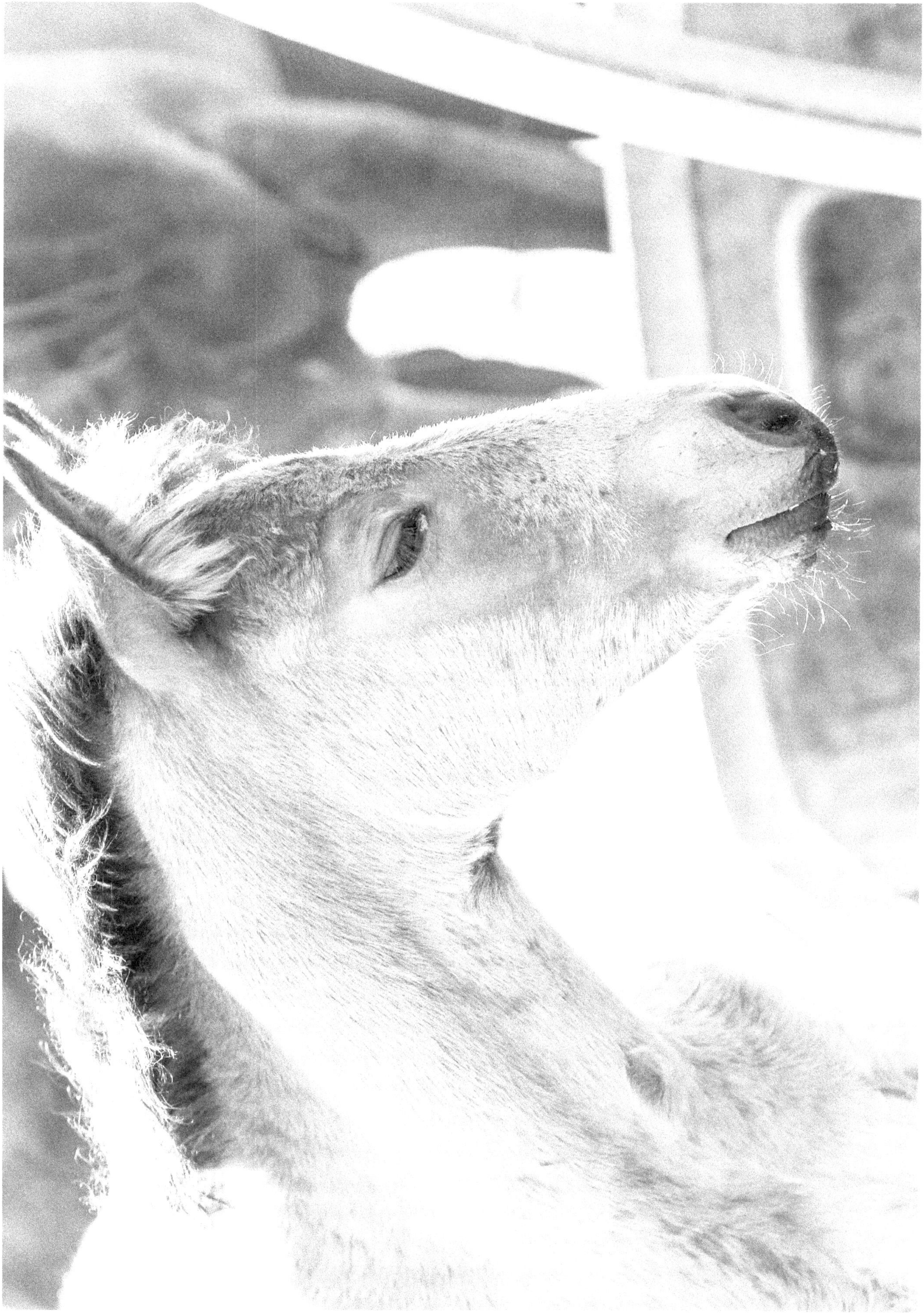

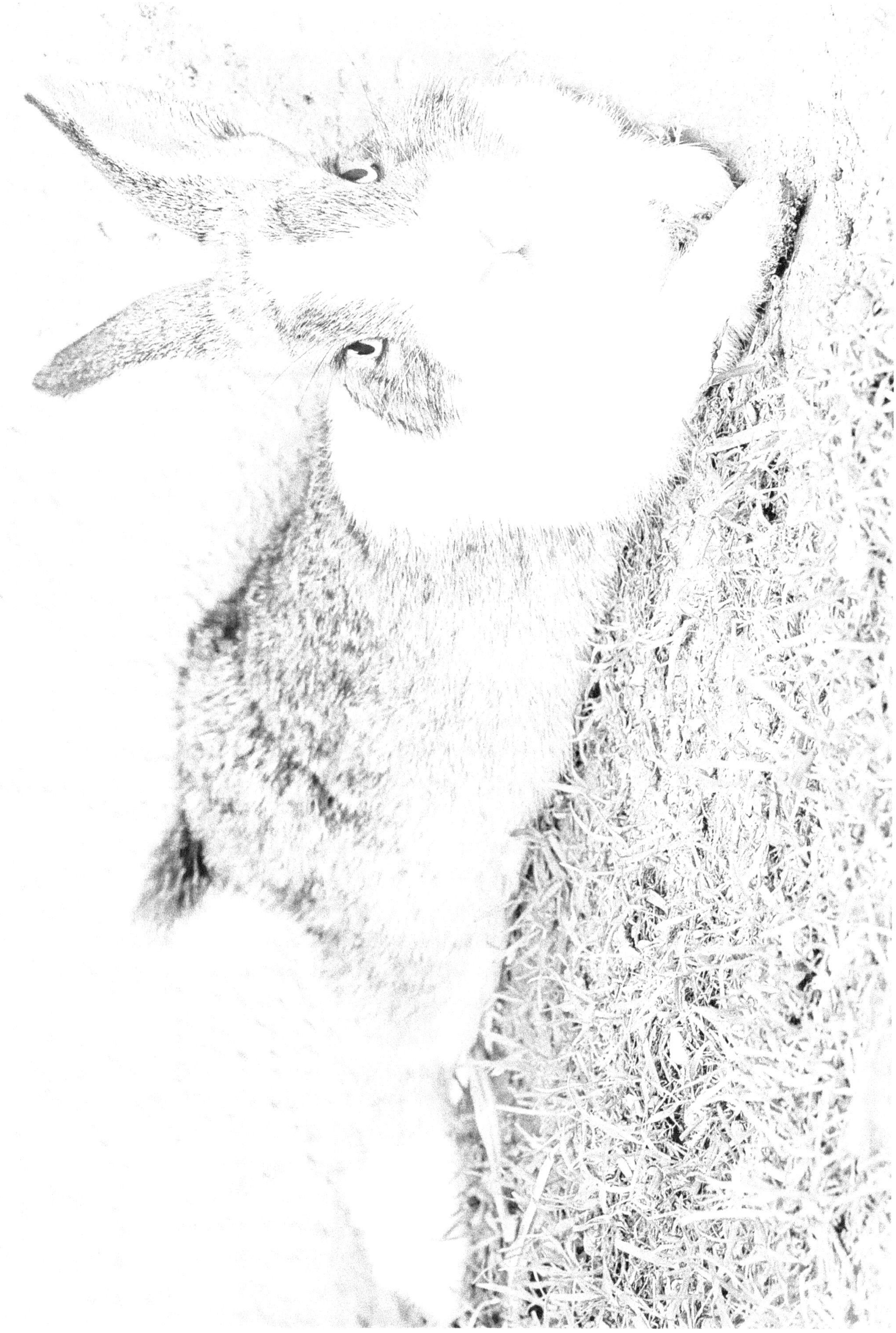

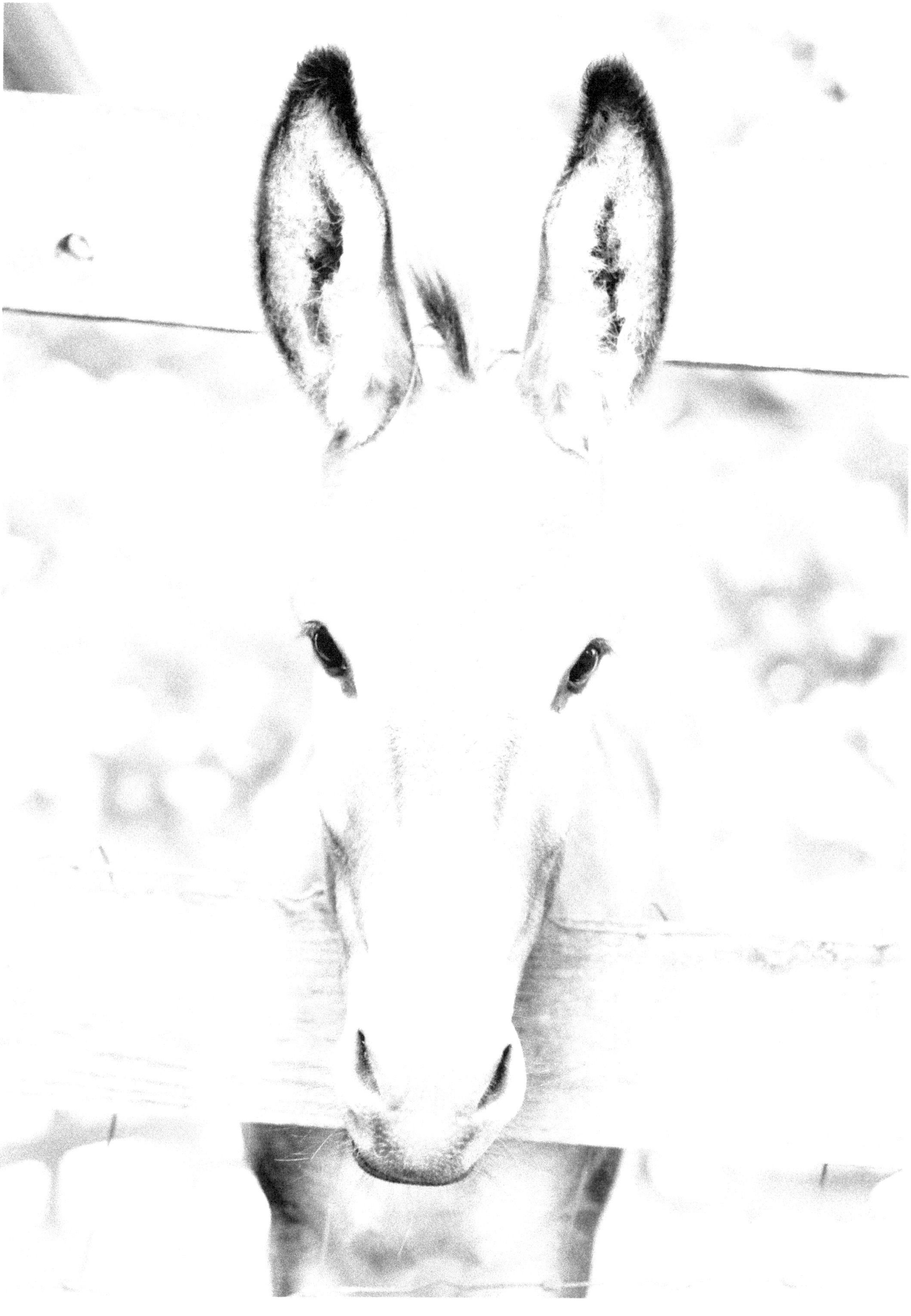

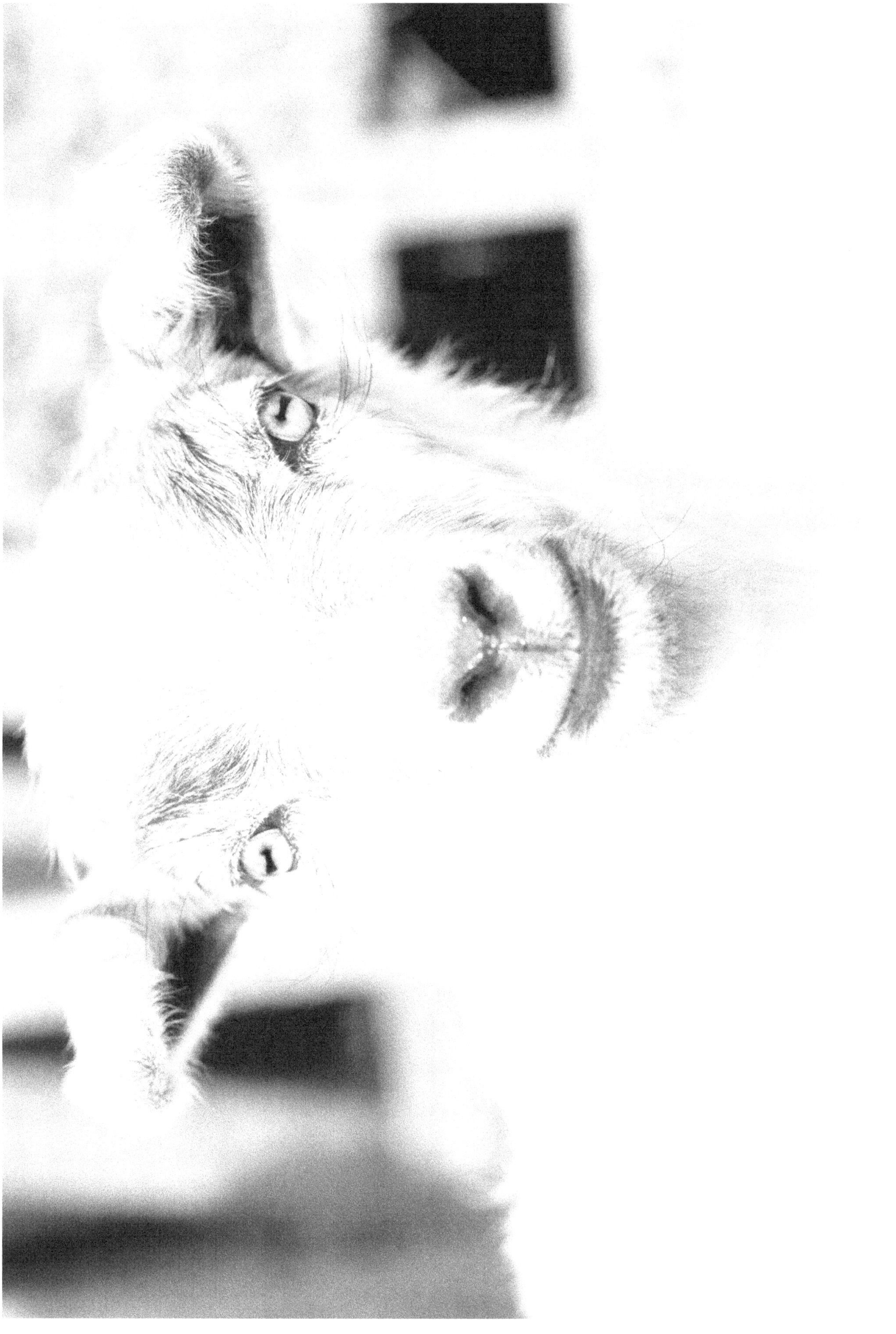

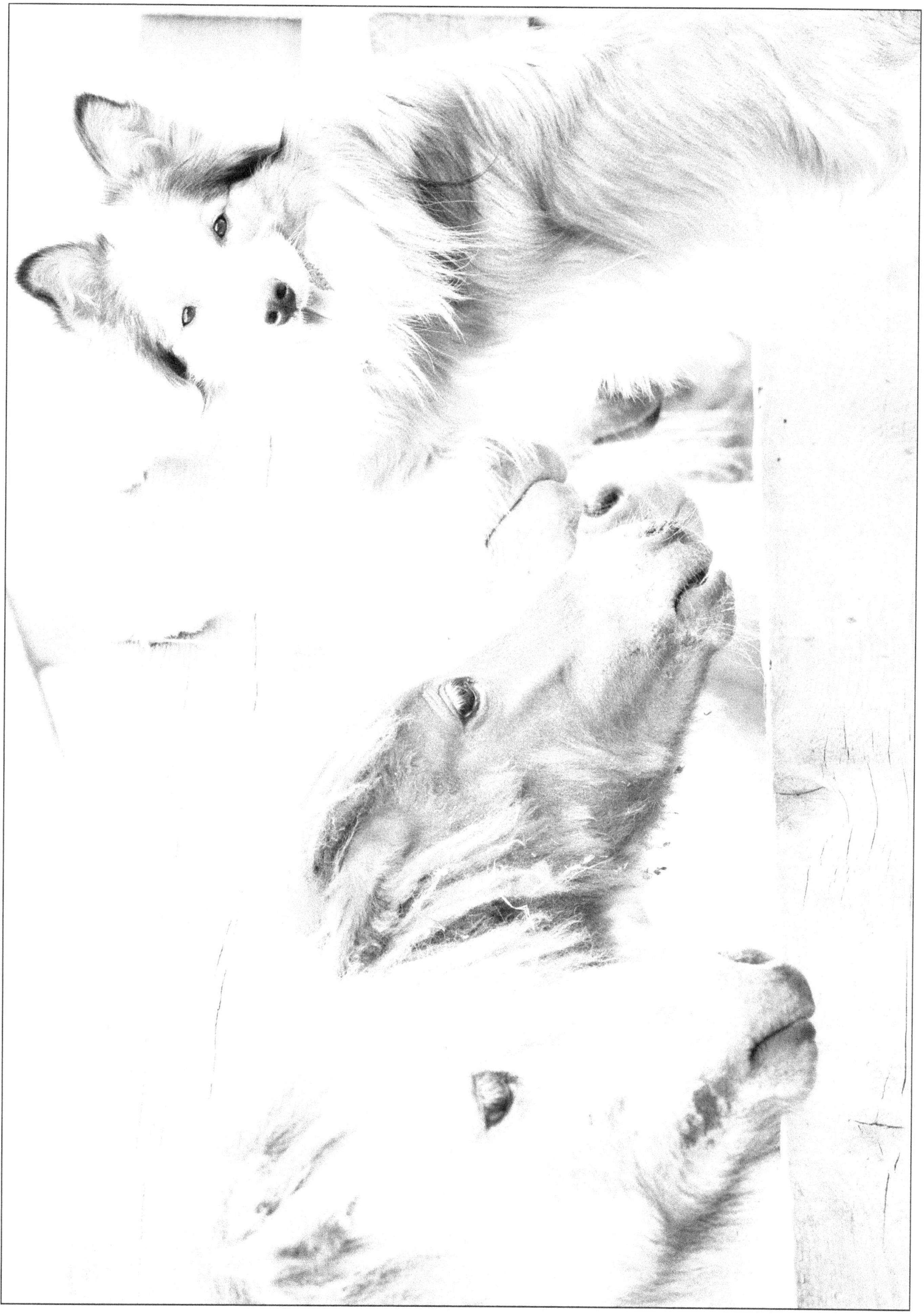

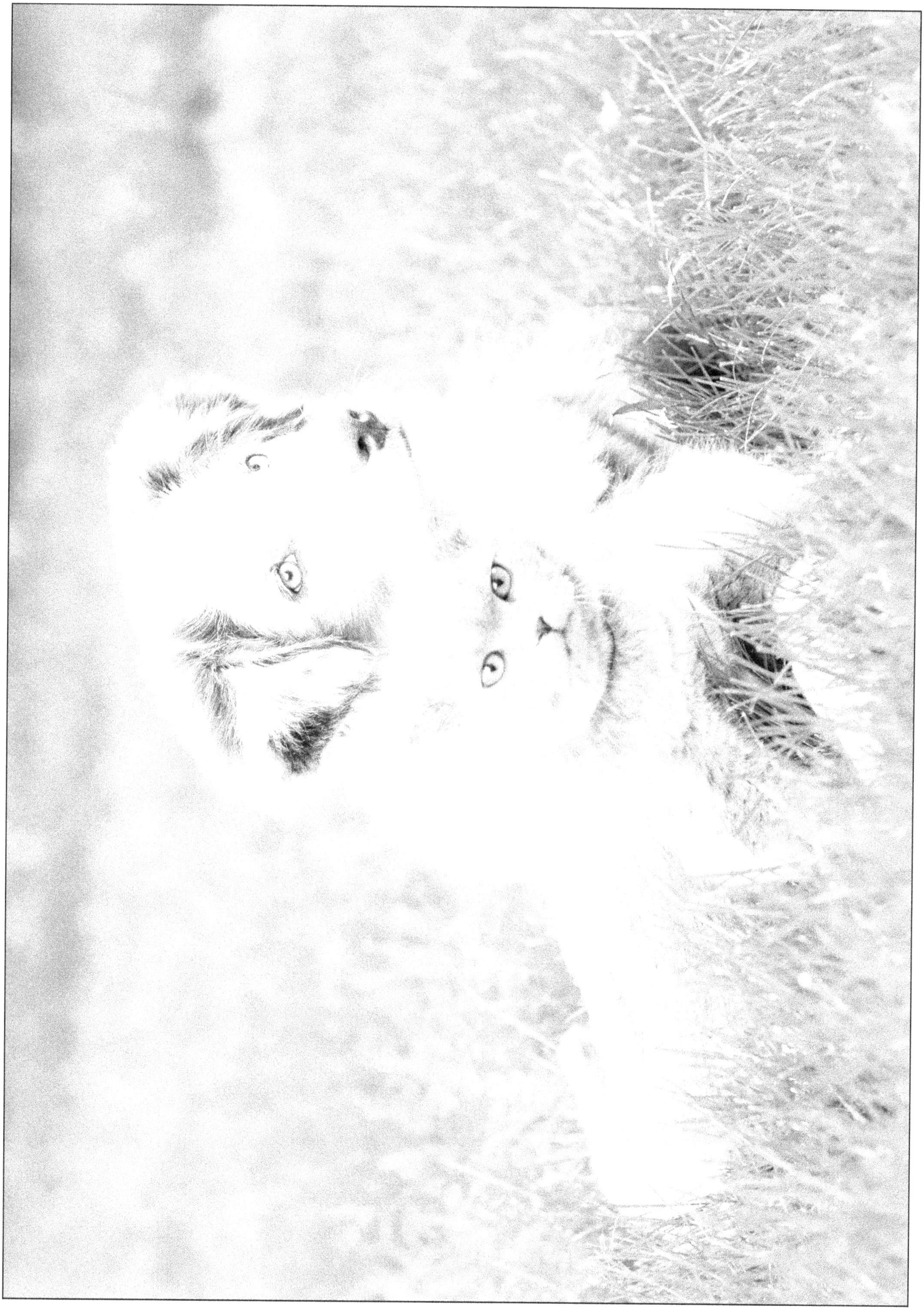

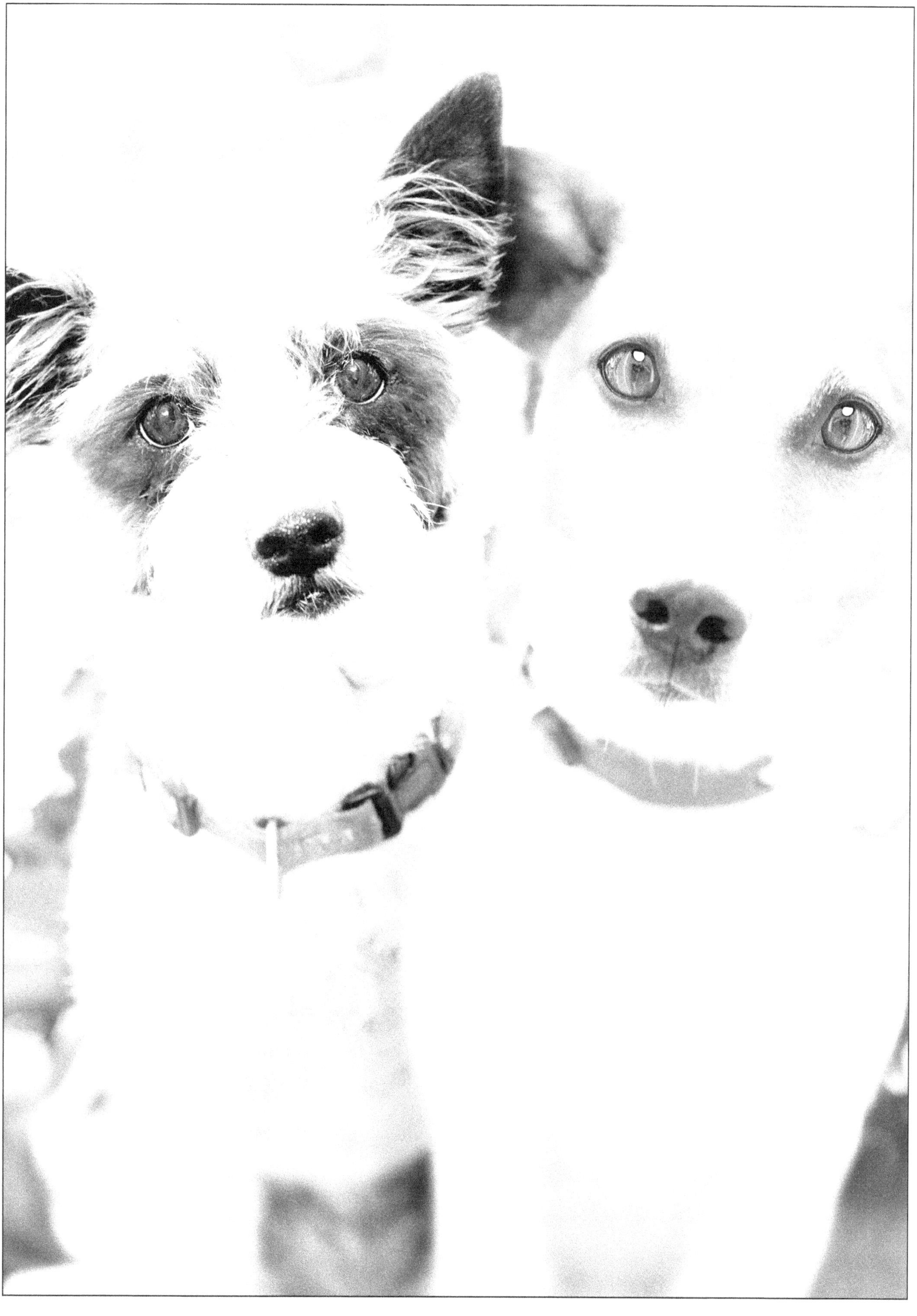

www.ingramcontent.com/pod-product-compliance
Lightning Source LLC
Chambersburg PA
CBHW080540190526
45169CB00007B/2572
* 9 7 8 1 5 3 2 8 5 9 5 9 5 *